NEWS BUREAUS
IN THE U.S.

Edited By

RICHARD WEINER

Seventh Edition

Other books by Richard Weiner

Professional's Guide to Public Relations Services
Professional's Guide to Publicity
Syndicated Columnists
Military Publications
College Alumni Publications
Investment Newsletters

Library of Congress Catalog Card Number: 80-83995
ISBN 0-913046-019

Printed in the United States of America
Published by
Public Relations Publishing Company
888 Seventh Ave., New York, N.Y. 10106
(212) 582-7373

In 1983, several major daily newspapers opened major news bureaus in cities far removed from their headquarters. The Chicago Tribune, Los Angeles Times, Washington Post, Dallas Morning News and Dallas Times-Herald considerably increased their national news coverage via bureaus in New York City and various regional media centers, such as Atlanta, Denver and Los Angeles.

Gannett's colorful innovation, USA Today, operates with a large staff in northern Virginia plus bureaus throughout the country. Circulations is well over a million.

In 1983, The Wall Street Journal passed the two-million mark. One of the main reasons for the phenomenal success of The Journal is its sizeable news staff, located in every one of the top 10 cities, and elsewhere.

With a 1983 circulation close to a million, the New York Post continued its circulation gains. Circulation increases also were posted in 1983 by The New York Times, Detroit News, Detroit Free Press, Newsday, Cleveland Plain Dealer, Houston Chronicle, Houston Post, Dallas Morning News and other daily newspapers.

In the 70's, many newspapers, troubled by circulation declines and cost increases, reduced the size and number of their bureaus. That trend definitely was reversed in the 80's. The trend to morning or all-day publication also continued. In early 1984, the St. Louis Post Dispatch switched from afternoon to morning publications. The only major afternoon dailies now are Newsday and the Milwaukee Journal!

Perhaps the most exciting development in 1983 with regard to news bureaus was the opening of many new bureaus by The Associated Press and United Press International. UPI thus not only survived but showed greater vitality than in the previous decade.

The field of trade, business and professional publications is more prosperous than ever before, particularly with the start of many new publications covering computers, telecommunications, health and marketing. Most of these publications operate with bureau systems.

In summary, news bureaus remain an important component of print journalism, with several bright developments.

Bureaus are branch editorial offices. It would be logical for cost accountants and efficiency experts to advocate consolidation. Though a few newspaper publishers have closed or relocated, most of them have improved local on-the-scene reporting, particularly in suburban areas. Many magazines are increasing their news coverage and quite a few now have bureaus, particularly in Atlanta, Houston and Los Angeles.

Take a look at the pages of Time and Newsweek on which the editorial personnel are listed. The largest section is the national and foreign bureau system. At Time, for example, over 20 people are in the Washington bureau, which is equal to the editorial staff of a small daily newspaper. Over a dozen reporters are in the Chicago and Los Angeles bureaus. In New York, Time maintains a local bureau in its headquarters building and also a bureau at the United Nations. All of this, plus bureaus in Atlanta, Boston, Denver, Detroit, Houston and San Francisco.

Among the daily newspapers, the largest bureau systems still are operated by The New York Times and Los Angeles Times. Both have extensive suburban operations, as well as bureaus throughout their states and the rest of the country.

Major bureau systems are not limited to the nation's top newspapers. The local bureau champs still are the Orlando Sentinel and Hartford Courant.

In a few cities, such as Chicago, newspapers are publishing more editions. The Chicago Tribune and Chicago Sun-Times are basically morning newspapers, but they now are called all-day newspapers because of late editions, which were added when the afternoon News folded.

Similarly, magazine publishers are striving to produce livelier products with more flexible closings and printing deadlines which permit late-breaking news from bureaus.

Advertisers are concerned with the quantity of circulation, and also the quality, that is, the buying power as reflected by income, education and other demographics. In most cases, the location of the news bureaus has been determined by the shift in the economic center of gravity from the inner city to the outer city, suburban and exurban areas.

Another new development is the assignment of specialized reporters within the bureaus. Specialists in business, fashion, restaurants and cultural activities now are located in suburban bureaus, as well as in Washington and other outlying bureaus.

For example, The Washington Post, USA Today and Los Angeles Times have business reporters in their New York City bureaus. Newsday, headquartered on Long Island, expanded its New York City bureaus in 1983, with news personnel added to its offices in Queens and Manhattan.

Yes, print journalism is alive and well in America in the 80's. This seventh edition of News Bureaus in the U.S. therefore is designed to be more useful than ever before to publicists, journalists and other readers. This edition reflects many hundreds of additions, deletions and changes, as compared to the previous edition.

More publications are listed than ever before. The text sections have been expanded, including circulation and other data about the leading newspaper in every state.

The greatest strength of the bureau system remains with daily newspapers and news services, and the net change here has been upward, in number of bureaus and personnel at each bureau. Many major newspapers have installed electronic and other data processing equipment to speed the increased transmission of news from suburban and state capital bureaus to the main news plant.

Several news services and syndicates are listed, with the private offices of major columnists. In addition, information about syndicated columnists is included in the listings of newspapers in New York, Miami, Chicago, Washington, Los Angeles and other cities which are the home base of columnists.

The annual Syndicate Directory of Editor & Publisher (the last issue in July) features a complete list of syndicates and columns by subject, title and author. However, most columnists are not located at the main offices of the syndicates, and we are plased to provide, in Syndicated Columnists and also in News Bureaus, the only directories which list the "home newspapers" or private offices of syndicated columnists.

This information is provided with the caution that syndicated colunists, as well as magazines, rarely use news releases and other mass-distributed material. A well-written letter to a columnist, offering an exclusive and demonstrating a familiarity with the type of column, is much preferred to a phone call or a news release or other mass mailing.

Another feature of News Bureaus in the U.S. is the list of *all* domestic bureaus of the Associated Press and United Press International. This data can be extremely useful, BUT it must be treated with respect. Publicists are urged not to send identical news releases to more than one bureau, and not to flood these, or any, bureaus with trivia.

Dow Jones, Fairchild and a few other news services and publications insist that publicists send news releases to the regional bureau in which the client or news source is located. This sometimes results in a problem for publicists outside of the Eastern time zone with regard to earnings or other timely releases which are issued late in the day. Western publicists and others who expect to issue "off-hours releases" can advise the regional bureau, which, in turn, will advise the headquarters bureau in New York. Except for major news, the New York City bureau generally will not respond until the regional bureau confirms and/or files a release.

The basic arrangement of the directory is an alphabetical list of states, and within each state, major publications are listed according to the city in which its editorial headquarters is located. To find the bureaus of a publication, check the index in the back of the book to determine the page number, or look within the book under the state in which the publication is headquartered.

In addition, 23 cities have been selected as news bureau centers, and a complete list is provided of all bureaus in the city. Thus, *all* of the bureaus of The New York Times, for example, are listed in the New York City section, and, in addition, each bureau is listed in the following city sections: Albany, Atlanta, Boston, Chicago, Denver, Detroit, Houston, Los Angeles, Miami, New Orleans, Philadelphia, San Francisco, Trenton, and Washington, D.C.

The 23 key bureau cities are:

Albany, N.Y.	Los Angeles, Calif.
Atlanta, Ga.	Miami, Fla.
Austin, Tex.	New York, N.Y.
Boston, Mass.	Philadelphia, Pa.
Chicago, Ill.	Pittsburgh, Pa.
Cleveland, Ohio	Sacramento, Calif.
Columbus, Ohio	St. Louis, Mo.
Dallas, Tex.	San Francisco, Calif.
Denver, Colo.	Springfield, Ill.
Detroit, Mich.	Trenton, N.J.
Harrisburg, Pa.	Washington, D.C.
Houston, Tex.	

These cities were selected because each is a major state capital and/or a large city in which there are more than two bureaus.

Several trade and business publications have been added in this edition, as a result of queries from readers. The best way to keep up-to-date with any publication is to read it. This can be misleading in the case of various trade publications which publish, usually on the contents or editorial pages, names and addresses of "offices." These offices often are advertising sales offices and are not news bureaus. Every attempt has been made to eliminate stringers, as well as advertising representatives.

Newspapers in Miami, Nashville, San Francisco and other cities share printing, advertising or other facilities, and often are located in the same building, but are completely independent and competitive, and are separate with regard to corporate ownership and editorial departments, including news bureaus.

In a few cities, newspapers which are not under the same ownership join on Sundays. A major example is The San Francisco Examiner and Chronicle which is published on Sundays. Occasionally, a combined Sunday newspaper has a name which differs from its daily components. In Springfield, Mass., for example, the Springfield Sunday Republican emerges from the Springfield Daily News and The Springfield Union.

An important auxiliary in making maximum use of this book is a map of the United States. A newspaper which is located near a state border is likely to have one or more bureaus in the adjacent state. For example, a news release about an event in Indiana should be sent to the appropriate Indiana bureau of the nearby Louisville (Kentucky) Courier-Journal.

The publicity business is imprecise, extremely competitive, and it is more difficult than ever before for the average news release to be published. The professional public relations practitioner can operate more efficiently in several ways, starting with the quality of the news release. A major factor concerns the sending of a news release to all publications which might have an interest in the specific subject. Some publicists resolve this problem by mailng to a large number of publications, including many which are not likely to have an interest in the subject. This is wasteful, of course, and can produce ill will from the media.

A news release mailed early in the week with a Sunday release often is preferred by local bureaus. The reason for this is that Sunday editions cover larger areas and have larger circulations than during the week, and print more news from the bureaus.

The professional publicist should utilize mailing services which maintain comprehensive, up-to-date media lists, and also subscribe to media directories and other services which enable you to maintain your own lists. These services are described in detail in Professional's Guide to Public Relations Services.

One technique, which rarely is utilized, it to send news releases and other publicity material to the bureaus, rather than the main offices of publications. Perhaps the major reason for this omission is that information about bureaus is not easily available. A few newspapers list the street addresses of their bureaus, usually on the editorial page. However, telephone numbers and names of bureau chiefs usually are not included. Several of the magazines, such as Time and Newsweek, list bureau personnel, but not addresses.

Many states have a Legislative Correspondents Association, and lists can be obtained by calling the press room in the state capitol. These lists are particularly useful for media which maintain bureaus only during legislative sessions.

Many publicaitons maintain bureaus at the United Nations, and a few of these are listed in this directory, In most cases, however, the U.N. correspondent operates a "sub-bureau" and is akin to a City Hall or other reporter covering a specific beat, under the direction of the city editor or other supervisor.

All bureaus in our nation's capital are listed in the excellent Hudson's Washington News Media Contacts Directory.

In Washington, D.C. where there are more bureaus than any other city, more news bureaus are in the National Press Building than any other building. The zip code of this landmark, which is at 529 14 Street, N.W., is 20045.

Extensive renovations were made in this building in 1983 and 1984. Many bureaus were relocated to other floors. In several cases, the suite numbers in this directory already have been changed or will be changed as a result of this shuffle. Fortunately, the suite number is not essential in mailing material to these bureaus.

In most cities, the name of a major building is sufficient address and it is not necessary to add the street address. Small and medium-size daily newspapers can be addressed without using street addresses. The key part of the address is the zip code. A few new buildings in which publications are located still have not caught on with postal sorters. In New York, for example, it sometimes is preferable to note that One Dag Hammarskhold Plaza is 245 East 47 Street and One Astor Plaza is 1515 Broadway.

In 1980, the Post Office established new zip codes restricted to single major office buildings. For example, in midtown Manhattan 666 Fifth Avenue now is 10103 and 888 Seventh Avenue is10106.

A comprehensive directory of news bureaus of the United States not only fills a void among public relations and media directories, but is designed to be extremely useful to publicists, as well as the media.

Several newspapers have dropped their headquarters city from their names to reflect broader geographical coverage. For example, The Star-Ledger formerly was The Newark Star-Ledger and The Times-Union formerly was called the Albany Times-Union. The Record, formerly called the Bergen Record, still is headquartered in Hackensack in Bergen county, New Jersey, but its coverage includes adjacent Rockland county, across the state border in New York.

Many major newspapers have state, suburban and national news editors. A news release sent to the city editor may be referred to the proper editor. It usually is more efficient, and a saving in time, to send it to the local bureau. A few newspapers maintain bureaus but prefer that news releases and other communications be sent only to their main offices. Information about these exceptions is included in this directory.

We strongly emphasize and caution that news releases should not be sent to every bureau and also to the main office of a publication. This results in considerable confusion with operations which have a large number of bureaus, such as The Associated Press and United Press International.

The Wall Street Journal and the Fairchild publications, for example, are national newspapers with a large number of local bureaus which cover their territories with considerable diligence. Publicists therefore are again reminded to send news releases to the appropriate local bureau.

In addition to newspapers, news magazines, wire services and syndicates, this directory includes a few major business and trade publications and consumer magazines which maintain bureaus. It is important to repeat that the mastheads of many business publications list several addresses which often are advertising and business offices. News releases sent to such offices generally are thrown away and rarely are forwarded to the proper editorial office.

As might be expected, most major consumer magazines are not oriented to local news and do not maintain bureaus. Thus, such major magazines as Family Circle and Popular Science are not listed in this directory. Also excluded are most of the medium-size and small circulation newspapers, though some of these maintain part-time bureaus in their state capitals during the legislative session.

A few large circulation magazines, including McCall's and Ladies' Home Journal, issue regional sections with local interest features. However, these sections are produced at the main offices. (Among the many media directories, the most comprehensive listing of personnel at national and local media which are headquartered in the New York City area is New York Publicity Outlets, published in Washington Depot, Connecticut 06794.)

This directory does not include the broadcast media. The networks and a few stations maintain bureaus, but their total number is considerably less than the print media.

An attempt also has been made to omit stringers, correspondents or part-time editorial personnel.

The definition of what constitutes a news bureau varies. The New York Times bureau in Washington, for example, is equal in size to the entire staff of a small city daily newspaper, while the bureaus of some newspapers consist of one person working at home.

Bureau personnel are changed more frequently than departmental editors or other staff members, and, in many cases, it is proper and preferable to address news releases to Bureau Chief rather than an individual name.

Changes in news bureau personnel are included in the newsletters sent to subscribers of Business Wire (235 Montgomery Street, San Francisco 94104) and Hudson's Washington News Media Contacts Directory (2626 Pennsylvania Ave., N.W., Washington, D.C. 20037).

We hope that the directory will be useful to public relations practitioners, and request comments, notations of errors and suggestions, which will be utilized in future editions.

It is in a spirit of mutual service to publicists and journalists that this book is directed.

The data for this directory was collected by hundreds of telephone calls and extensive correspondence. As with any directory, this book includes errors, typographical and otherwise, for which the author humbly assumes responsibility.

Readers are asked to send corrections and suggestions to the author.

ALABAMA

BIRMINGHAM NEWS

Box 2553, Birmingham 35202

(205) 325-2222

The evening News is the state's largest circulation newspaper—164,000 daily and 210,000 Sunday—considerably more than the morning Post-Herald, which is the second in the state (66,000).

The News operates bureaus in Bessemer, Pelham and Center Point. News releases for these areas should be sent to Orbie Medders, metropolitan editor.

Anniston:

105 Pokono Dr., Ohatchee 36271

(205) 892-3353, Kaye Dickie

Huntsville:

2013 Broadman St., Huntsville

(205) 536-6207, Matt Moffett

Mobile:

1455 Long Wood Road, Mobile 36609

(205) 343-0155, Sandra Baxley Taylor

Montgomery:

Whitley Hotel, Montgomery 36104

(205) 262-6461 Sam Duval

Washington, D.C.:

1750 Pennsylvania Ave. N.W., Wash., D.C. 20006

(202) 383-7800, Tom Scarritt (Newhouse News Service)

BIRMINGHAM POST-HERALD

Box 2553, Birmingham 35202

(205) 325-2342

Montgomery:

304 Cullen, Montgomery 36104

(205) 264-0921, Frank Bruer

Washington, D.C.:

1110 Vermont Avenue, N.W., Wash., D.C. 20005

(202) 833-9520, Gayle McCracken

ALASKA

ANCHORAGE DAILY NEWS

200 Potter Dr., Anchorage 99502

(907) 786-4200

Alaska's only morning newspaper, The Anchorage Daily News considerably increased its daily circulation in 1983 to 51,000, the largest in the state. On Sundays, the News has a circulation of 54,000, which is smaller than

its arch-rival, The Times. In addition to bureaus in Juneau and Kenai, the News has a bureau in Mat-Su, headed by Doug O'Harra, who is reached via the Anchorage Daily News main office.
Juneau:
> Capitol Press Room, Juneau 99811
> (907) 586-9571

Kenai:
> Box 4196, Kenai 99611
> (907) 283-3094

Washington, D.C.:
> 203 "C" Street, N.E., Washington, D.C. 20002
> (202) 547-4077, Karin Davies

ARIZONA

THE ARIZONA REPUBLIC
> 120 E. Van Buren St., Phoenix 85004
> (602) 271-8000

The Arizona Republic operates bureaus in Flagstaff, Kingman, Prescott and Tucson. However, news releases should be sent to the State Desk.

Circulation is the largest in the state—up in 1983 to an all-time high of 385,000 daily and 410,000 Sunday.
Flagstaff:
> 1105 E. Ponderosa Pkwy., #232,
> (602) 774-8912, John Schroeder

Kingman:
> Box 3056, Kingman 86401
> (602 753-5839, Steve Daniels

Tucson:
> 4500 W. Speedway Blvd., Tucson 85704
> (602) 622-4922, Gen Varn

Washington, D.C.:
> 641 Ntl. Press Bldg., Wash., D.C. 20045
> (202) 638-6425, Benjamin R. Cole, Anne Q. Hoy

THE PHOENIX GAZETTE
> 120 E. Van Buren St., Phoenix 85004
> (602) 271-8000

Washington, D.C.:
> 641 Ntl. Press Bldg., Wash., D.C. 20045
> (202) 638-6425, Sean Griffin

TUCSON CITIZEN

Box 26767, Tucson 85776

(602) 573-4400

Phoenix:

The Press Room, Senate Wing, 1700 W. Washington, Phoenix 85007

(604) 255-5813, Shawn Hubler

ARKANSAS

DONREY MEDIA GROUP

920 Rogers Ave., Fort Smith 72901

(501) 785-7700

39 daily and 35 weekly newspapers in Arkansas, California, Hawaii, Indiana, Kentucky, Missouri, Nevada, Oklahoma, Texas and Washington. The flagship newspaper is The Southwest Times Record in Fort Smith.

Nevada:

Nevada Appeal, 200 Bath St., Carson City 89701

(702) 882-2111, Terry Wade

Washington, D.C.:

1068 Ntl. Press Bldg., Wash., D.C. 20045

(202) 787-1760, Eric Ruff

ARKANSAS DEMOCRAT

Capitol Ave. and Scott, Little Rock 72203

(501) 378-3400

Benton:

1211 W. South St., Benton 72015

(501) 778-4853, P.J. Spaul

Conway:

201 Parkway Office Bldg., 809 Parkway, Conway 72032

(501) 329-8553, Mark Carponis

Little Rock:

Press Rm., State Capitol, Little Rock 72203

(501) 378-3438

Pine Bluff:

715 Popular St., Pine Bluff 71601

(501) 536-2285, Larry Sullivan

ARKANSAS GAZETTE

112 W. Third Ave., Little Rock 72203

(501) 376-6161

The morning Gazette has the state's largest circulation, 128,000 daily and 155,000 Sunday.

3

Washington, D.C.:
> 605 14th St., N.W., Wash., D.C. 20004
> (202) 347-9403, Carol Matlack

CALIFORNIA

THE FRESNO BEE
> 1626 E St., Fresno 93786
> (209) 441-6111

Capital:
> 925 L St., Suite 340, Sacramento 95814
> (916) 446-9363, Ed Salzman

Washington, D.C.:
> 203 C St., N.E., Wash., D.C. 20002
> (202) 547-4044, Leo Rennert, John Johnson, Jeff Raimundo
> and
> Senate Press Gallery, U.S. Capitol, Wash., D.C. 20510
> (202) 224-0241 (McClatchy Newspapers)

FIELD NEWSPAPER SYNDICATE
> 1703 Kaiser Ave., Irvine 92714
> (714) 549-8700

New York:
> 30 E. 42 St., N.Y. 10017
> (212) 682-5560

Field Newspaper Syndicate, formerly Publishers-Hall, also distributes Independent Press, a news service, headquartered at The Chicago Sun-Times, 401 N. Wabash Ave., Chicago 60611, with Krshna K. Guar as Director.

> Following are the offices of a few of the columnists.
> Others, including Ann Landers and Sidney J. Harris, are at the Chicago Sun-Times, or can be reached via the syndicate office.
> Betty Beale, 2926 Garfield St., N.W., Wash., D.C. 20008, (202) 232-3525
> Rowland Evans, Jr. and Robert D. Novak, 1750 Pennsylvania Ave., N.W., Wash., D.C. 20006, (202) 393-4340
> Hy and Marilyn Gardner, 1111 Brickell Ave., Miami, Fla. 33131, (305) 377-0811
> Joseph A. Livingston, Philadelphia Inquirer, 400 N. Broad St., Philadelphia, Pa. 19101, (215) 854-2077
> Victor Riesel, 30 E. 42 St., N.Y. 10017, (212) 682-3337
> Carl T. Rowan, 3251-C Sutton Pl., Wash., D.C. 20016, (202) 966-8668
> Jimmy (The Greek) Snyder, Box 976, N. Miami Beach, Fla. 33160, (305) 445-3702

LONG BEACH PRESS-TELEGRAM
604 Pine Ave., Long Beach 90844

(213) 435-1161

Sacramento:

345 Park Executive Bldg., 925 L St., Sacramento 95814

(916) 322-3022, Bob Schmidt (also San Jose Mercury and News)

Washington, D.C.:

1319 F St., N.W., Wash., D.C. 20004

(202) 637-3621, Carl Cammon

LOS ANGELES

THE APPAREL NEWS GROUP
945 South Wall St., Los Angeles 90015

(213) 626-0411, (800) 421-8867

California Fashion Publications Inc. (The Apparel News Group)
publishes national and regional magazines in the men's and women's apparel
fields—Apparel News South (formerly Atlanta Apparel News), Bridal Apparel
News, California Apparel News, California Men's Stylist, Chicago Apparel
News, Dallas Apparel News, Men's Apparel News and New York Apparel
News.

Atlanta:

Atlanta Apparel Mart, 250 Spring St., N.W., Atlanta 30303

(404) 688-6830, Leslie Bayer

Chicago:

The Apparel Center, 350 N. Orleans, Chicago 60654

(312) 670-2230, Paula Lashinsky

Dallas:

2300 Stemmons, Dallas 75258

(214) 634-8315, Susan Roche

New York:

110 W. 40 St., N.Y. 10018

(212) 221-8288, David Moin

AUTOMOTIVE AGE
Box 2006, 6931 Van Nuys Blvd., Van Nuys 91405

(213) 873-1320

Bureaus in Chicago, Detroit and Washington, D.C., but editor Chris
Hosford requests that releases be sent to California.

BON APPETIT
5900 Wilshire Blvd., Los Angeles 90036

(213) 937-1025

New York:

9 W. 57 St., N.Y. 10019

(212) 753-6683, Ms. Zack Hanle

DAILY NEWS

Box 400, Los Angeles 90051

(213) 997-4111

The Los Angeles Daily News started as a controlled circulation six-day newspaper in Van Nuys, where it was called the Valley News. This extra-ordinary successful suburban newspaper now is published seven mornings and has a daily paid circulation of 135,000 and Sunday circulation of 151,000.
Los Angeles:

Room 338, City Hall, 200 N. Spring St., Los Angeles 90012

(213) 485-3720, Joyce Peterson

Room 485F, County Hall of Administration, 500 W. Temple St., Los Angeles 90012, (213) 974-8985

Sacramento:

925 L St., Sacramento 95814

(916) 446-6723, Bill Packer

EAST/WEST NETWORK

5900 Wilshire Blvd., Los Angeles 90036

(213) 937-5810

East/West publishes the inflight magazines of several major airlines, with a combined circulation of about a million. The field has become extremely competitive. Other inflight publishers are North/South Network in Miami and Webb in St. Paul, as well as individual airlines, including American.
New York:

34 E. 51 St., N.Y. 10022

(212) 888-5900

HOLLYWOOD REPORTER

6715 Sunset Blvd., Hollywood 90028

(213) 464-7411

New York:

1501 Broadway, N.Y. 10036

(212) 354-1858, Mitchell Hall, Sharon Dobular

Washington, D.C.:

1234 Ntl. Press Bldg., Wash., D.C. 20045

(202) 737-2828, Theresa McMasters

LOS ANGELES HERALD EXAMINER

Box 2416, 1111 S. Broadway, Los Angeles 90015

(213) 748-1212

The largest circulation (278,000) newspaper in the Hearst chain, the Los Angeles Herald Examiner provides material to the other Hearst newspapers in Albany, Baltimore, San Antonio, San Francisco and Seattle. Among its columnists who are syndicated are James Bacon (Hollywood) and Melvin Durslag (sports).

Unlike the Los Angeles Times, the Herald Examiner does not operate with a bureau system.

Washington, D.C.:

1701 Pennsylvania Ave., N.W., Wash., D.C. 20006

(202) 298-6920, Joseph Kingsbury Smith

LOS ANGELES TIMES

Times-Mirror Sq., Los Angeles 90053

(213) 972-5000

California

Orange County Edition:

1375 Sunflower Ave., Costa Mesa 92626

(714) 957-2000, Narda Zaccino

Sacramento:

925 L St., Sacramento 95814

(916) 445-8860, William Endicott

San Diego County Edition:

225 Broadway, San Diego 9210?

(714) 238-1617, Dale Fetherling (Tom Goff is bureau chief)

San Francisco:

825 Fox Plaza, San Francisco 94102

(415) 431-1600

San Bernardino-Riverside:

The Mission Inn, Riverside 92501

(714) 794-3820, Wes Hughes

Santa Barbara:

924 Anacapa St., Santa Barbara 93101

(805) 963-1357, John Hurst

National

Chicago:

435 N. Michigan Ave., Chicago 60611

(312) 467-4670, Larry Green

Denver:

1415 Larimer Square, Denver 80202

(303) 825-2345, Bill Curry

Detroit:

615 Griswald St., Detroit 48226

(313) 965-4570, Donald Woutat

Houston:

Chronicle Bldg., Houston 77002

(713) 237-0808, Rone Tempest

Miami:

3000 Biscayne Blvd., Miami 33137

(305) 757-1531, Barry Bearak

New York:

220 E. 42 St., N.Y. 10017

(212) 661-7110, John Goldman

Washington, D.C.:

1875 Eye St., N.W., Wash., D.C. 20006

(202) 293-4650, Jack Nelson

In 1983, Norman Miller, long-time Washington Bureau chief of the Wall Street Journal, moved west to become national editor of the L.A. Times.

In addition to the three daily editions (Metro, Orange County and San Diego County) the Times publishes six suburban sections. (Five are published semi-weekly and one is published weekly.) The suburban bureaus are:

Glendale/Burbank:

401 N. Brand Blvd., Glendale 91203

972-7124

San Fernando Valley ("The Valley"):

Box 7457, Van Nuys 91409

San Gabriel:

9159 E. La Rosa Dr., Temple City 91780

287-0491

South Bay:

2908 182 St., Redondo Beach 90278

752-5053

Southeast/Long Beach:

8301 E. Florence Ave., Downers 90240

993-9711

West Side:

2716 Ocean Park Blvd., Santa Monica 90405

450-6666

The nation's second largest circulation daily newspaper, The Los Angeles Times had a 1983 circulation of 1,038,000 daily and 1,294,000 Sunday.

The Times publishes five semi-weekly suburban sections (Centinela-South Bay, San Gabriel Valley, Southeast, San Fernando Valley, West Side) and one weekly suburban section (Glendale-Burbank). Rather than dealing with these separate offices, publicists can send releases to Robert Ravitch, suburban editor, at Times-Mirror Square.

The Times has 20 foreign bureaus and seven domestic bureaus, including a staff of 39 in Washington, D.C. State bureaus are located in Sacramento, San Bernardino, Riverside, San Francisco and Santa Barbara.

The Times also operates a news service with The Washington Post at 1150 15th St., N.W., Washington, D.C. 20071, (202) 334-6173. Times staff members who are syndicated include Jim Murray (sports), Roderick Mann (entertainment), Paul Conrad (editorial cartoons), Paul Henninger (television), Carolyn Murray (home) and Marylou Lou Luther (fashion). Syndicated columnists with their own offices in the capital include:

Art Buchwald, 1750 Pennsylvania Ave., N.W., Wash., D.C. 20006, (202) 393-6680

Georgie Anne Geyer, 1006 The Plaza, 800 25th St., N.W., Wash., D.C. 20037, (202) 333-9176

Nick Thimmesch, 6301 Broadbranch Rd., Chevy Chase, MD 20015, (303) 652-1588

Following are the private office addresses of syndicated columnists at other locations.

Paul Harvey, 360 N. Michigan Ave., Chicago 60601, (312) 263-0800

Jenkin Lloyd Jones, Tulsa World, Tulsa 74102, (918) 582-1101

Neil Solomon, M.D., 1726 Reistertown Rd., Baltimore 21208, (301) 484-3080

RACQUETBALL ILLUSTRATED

7011 Sunset Blvd., Hollywood 90028

(213) 467-1300

Contributing editors at several newspapers, but no bureaus.

TEEN

8490 Sunset Blvd., Los Angeles 90069

(213) 657-5100

New York:

437 Madison Ave., N.Y. 10022

(212) 935-9150, Hollie Alper

The editorial staff of this monthly magazine is divided between the Los Angeles headquarters of Peterson Publishing Company and the New York branch office. New York editors include beauty and fashion.

LOS ANGELES BUREAUS (area code 213)

Advertising Age, 6404 Wilshire Blvd., L.A. 90048, Morrie Gelman, 651-3710

Amusement Business, 9107 Wilshire Blvd., L.A. 90210, Linda Deckard, 237-7040

Associated Press, 1111 S. Hill Street, L.A. 90015, 746-1200

Automotive News, 6404 Wilshire Blvd., L.A. 90048, Matt De Lorenzo, 651-3710

Aviation Week & Space Technology, 3333 Wilshire Blvd., L.A. 90010, Robert R. Ropelewski, 487-1160

Back Stage, 5670 Wilshire Blvd., L.A. 90036, Bob Harris, 936-5200

Billboard, 9107 Wilshire Blvd., Beverly Hills 90210, Lee Zhito, Sam Sutherland, 273-7040

Broadcasting, 1680 N. Vine Street, Hollywood 90028, Richard Mahler, 436-3148

Business Insurance, 6404 Wilshire Blvd., L.A. 90048, Rhonda J. Rundle, 651-3710

Business Week, 3200 Wilshire Blvd., L.A. 90010, Stewart Toy, 487-1160

Capitol News Service, 1741 N. Ivar, L.A. 90028, 462-6371

Cash Box, 6363 Sunset Blvd., Hollywood 90028, Richard Imamuro, 464-8241

Chain Store Age, 606 N. Larchmont Blvd., L.A. 90035, Edith Myles, 559-5111

Chicago Tribune, 417 S. Hill St., L.A. 90013, Rogers Worthington, 624-5420

Christian Science Monitor, 5225 Wilshire Blvd., L.A. 90036, Marshall
   Ingersen, 932-1260

Electronics, 3200 Wilshire Blvd., South Tower, L.A. 90010, Larry Walter,
   487-1160

Fairchild Publications, 615 S. Flower St., L.A. 90017, Steve Ginsberg,
   624-1981

Forbes, 12233 W. Olympia Blvd., L.A. 90064, Laury Minard, 628-2344

Gralla Publications, 16200 Ventura Blvd., Encino 91438, 788-0271

Industry Week, 16255 Ventura Blvd., Encino 91436, Lad Kuzela, 990-9000

Iron Age, 6767 Forest Lawn Dr., L.A. 90068, A.M. Senita, 851-6500

Jet, 3600 Wilshire Blvd., L.A. 90010, Aldore Collier, 386-5200

McGraw-Hill World News Service, 3200 Wilshire, L.A. 90010, Barbara Lamb,
   487-1160

Medical World News, 3612 Hamilton St., Irvine 92714, Richard Trubo,
   (714) 552-4481

Merchandising, 16200 Ventura Blvd., Encino 91436, Deborah Cromer,
   788-0271

Multichannel News, 615 S. Flower Street, L.A. 90017, Stewart Schley,
   624-1981

New York Times, 900 Wilshire Blvd., L.A. 90017, Bob Lindsey, 624-2349

Newspaper Enterprise Association, 1665 N. Beverly Dr., Beverly Hills
   90210, Dick Kleiner, 271-0136

Newsweek, 10100 Santa Monica Blvd., L.A. 90067, Janet Huck, 553-3059

Official Airline Guides, 1717 N. Highland Ave., L.A. 90028, Gerald Orlin,
   466-3265

Penthouse, 924 Westwood Blvd., L.A. 90024, 496-6100

People, 450 N. Roxbury Dr., Beverly Hills 90210, 273-1530

Philadelphia Inquirer, c/o L.A. Examiner, Box 2416, Terminal Annex, L.A.
   90051, Larry Eichel, 749-1747

Playboy, 8560 Sunset Blvd., L.A. 90048, 659-4080

Reuters, 3407 W. 6th Street, L.A. 90020, Ronald C. Clarke, 380-2014

Rolling Stone, 1 Century Plaza, 2029 Century Park E., L.A. 90067, 553-9414

Sports Illustrated, 280 S. Beverly Dr., Beverly Hills 90212, Denise Hall,
   858-1591

TV Guide, 9000 Sunset Blvd., L.A. 90036, Steve Gelman, 276-0676

Time, 450 N. Roxbury Dr., Beverly Hills 90210, Benjamin Cate, 273-1530

Travel Weekly, 3460 Wilshire Blvd., Beverly Hills 90010, Jerry Brown,
   387-2100

**Travelage East, Travelage Southeast, Travel Management Daily,
   Travel Management Newsletter,** 2999 Overland Ave., L.A. 90064,
   Gerald Orlin, Lorraine June, 204-1184

U.S. News & World Report, 9465 Wilshire Blvd., Beverly Hills 90212, Juanita
    R. Hogue, 274-9404

USA Today, 924 Westwood Blvd., L.A. 90024, Eric Brazil, 208-6425

United Press International, 316 West 2nd Street, L.A. 90012, 620-1230

Us, 9441 Wilshire Blvd., Beverly Hills 90212, Rana Arons, 273-1081

Variety, 1400 N. Cahuenga Blvd., Hollywood 90028, Thomas M. Pryor,
    469-1141

Wall Street Journal, 514 Shatto Pl., L.A. 90020, Barney Calame, 383-9090

Washington Post, 10100 Santa Monica Blvd., Century City 90067, 277-4819

THE TRIBUNE

    Box 24424, Oakland 94623

    (415) 645-2000,

    During the last few years, the Oakland Tribune became East Bay
Today (a Gannett newspaper) and then returned to independent status as The
Tribune. Through these various changes, Robert C. Maynard remained as
editor. Circulation now is 179,000 (morning) and 168,000 (Sunday). The
newspaper is in Alameda County, across the Bay from San Francisco.
Sacramento:

    Park Executive Bldg., 925 L St., Rm. 385, Sacramento 95814

    (916) 445-5424, Virgil Meibert

PRESS-ENTERPRISE

    Box 792, 14 and Orange Grove, Riverside 92501

    (714) 684-1200

    The morning Enterprise (circulation 75,000) and evening Press
(34,000) combine as the Sunday Press-Enterprise (114,000). Extensive
coverage of Riverside County is provided by six bureaus. Bob Marshall is
county editor.
Banning:

    3166 W. Ramsey, Banning 92220

    (714) 849-4531, Bob Pratte

Corona:

    712 Main Street, Corona 91720

    (714) 737-1313, Iris Hayward

Hemet:

    25135 San Jacinto St., Hemet 92343

    (714) 658-4455, Darrell Santschi

Indio:

    45015 Oasis St., Indio 92201

    (619) 347-3494, Mike Kataoka

Palm Desert:

    74405 Highway III, Palm Desert 92260

    (619) 346-1181

Palm Springs:
>   1534 N. Palm Canyon Dr., Palm Springs 92262
>   (619) 325-1151, Herb Pasik

Sacramento:
>   925 L St., Sacramento 95814
>   (916) 445-9973, Richard Zeiger

Sun City:
>   27070 Sun City Blvd., Sun City 92381
>   (714) 679-1191, Bill McKenna

Washington, D.C.:
>   14 Tenth St., Wash., D.C. 20002
>   (202) 546-1914, Martin Salditch

SACRAMENTO

CAPITOL NEWS SERVICE

>   1113 H St., Sacramento 95814
>   (916) 445-6336

Los Angeles:
>   1741 N. Ivar, Los Angeles 90028
>   (213) 462-6371

>   Executive offices are in Los Angeles, where Fred W. Kline is

executive editor.

SACRAMENTO BEE

>   Box 15779, 21st and Q, Sacramento 95852
>   (916) 446-9611

Capital:
>   925 L St., Sacramento 95814
>   (916) 446-9357, Ted Sell

Washington, D.C.:
>   203 C St., N.E., Wash., D.C. 2000?

>   (202) 547-4044, Leo Rennert, Richard Hall, John Johnson, Jeff
Raimundo. Also at Senate Press Gallery, U.S. Capitol, Wash., D.C. 20510,
(202) 224-0241

>   Headquartered in Sacramento and headed by C.K. McClatchy,
president and editor, the McClatchy newspapers are The Fresno Bee, The
Modesto Bee and The Sacramento Bee, all in central and northern California,
and all morning newspapers.

SACRAMENTO UNION

>   301 Capitol Mall, Sacramento 95812
>   (916) 442-7811

Sacramento:
> 925 L St., Sacramento 95814
> (916) 442-7811, Dan Walters

SACRAMENTO BUREAUS (area code 916)

Associated Press, 927 L St., Sacramento 95814, 448-9555
Daily Journal, 1190 Park Executive Bldg., 925 L Street, Sacramento 95814, Robert Studer, 443-4494
Daily News, 925 L Street, Sacramento 95814, Bill Parker, 446-6723
Fresno Bee, 925 L St., Sacramento 95814, Ed Salzman, 446-9363
Long Beach Press-Telegram, 345 Park Executive Bldg., 925 L St., Sacramento 95814, Bob Schmidt, 322-3022
Los Angeles Times, 925 L St., Sacramento 95814, William Endicott, 445-8860
Press-Enterprise, 925 L St., Sacramento 95814, Richard Zeiger, 445-9973
San Diego Union, 925 L St., Sacramento 95814, Daniel S. Carson, 925-6510
San Francisco Chronicle, 925 L St., Sacramento 95814, Gale Cook, 455-5658
San Francisco Examiner, 925 L St., Sacramento 95814, Steve Capps, 445-4310
San Jose Mercury News, 925 L St., Sacramento 95814, Sam Meyes, 441-4601
Tribune, 925 L St., Sacramento 95814, Ron Roach, 445-6510
United Press International, 925 L St., Sacramento 95814, 445-7755

THE TRIBUNE

> 350 Camino de la Reina, San Diego 92108
> (619) 299-3131

Sacramento:
> 925 L St., Sacramento 95814
> (916) 445-6510, Ron Roach

Capital:
> 925 L St., Sacramento 95814
> (916) 446-9357, Ted Sell

Washington, D.C.:
> 203 C St., N.E., Wash., D.C. 2000?
> (202) 547-4044, Leo Rennert, Richard Hall, John Johnson, Jeff

Raimundo. Also at Senate Press Gallery, U.S. Capitol, Wash., D.C. 20510, (202) 224-0241

Washington, D.C.:
> 1100 Ntl. Press Bldg., Wash., D.C. 20045
> (202) 737-6960, George Condon

The Tribune, which has a circulation of 127,000 is a Copley newspaper. The Copley bureaus are listed under the San Diego Union.

SAN DIEGO UNION

350 Camino de la Reina, San Diego 92108

(714) 299-3131

Sacramento:

925 L St., Sacramento 95814

(916) 445-6510, Daniel C. Carson

Washington, D.C.:

1100 Ntl. Press Bldg., Wash., D.C. 20045

(202) 737-6960, L. Edgar Prina

Copley Newspapers, headquartered in San Diego, operates Copley News Service which links its newspapers. The largest circulation is the San Diego Union — 230,000 daily and 344,000 Sunday, considerably higher than in previous years.

California

San Diego Tribune, 350 Camino de la Reina, San Diego 92108

(714) 299-3131

San Diego Union, 350 Camino de la Reina, San Diego 92108

(714) 299-3131

San Pedro News-Pilot, 356 Seventh St., San Pedro 90733

(213) 832-0221

South Bay Breeze, 5215 Torrance Blvd., Torrance 90503

(213) 370-5511

Illinois

Aurora Beacon-News, 101 S. River St., Aurora 60506

(312) 897-4241

Elgin Courier-News, 300 Lake St., Elgin 60120

(312) 741-1800

Joliet Herald-News, 78 N. Scott St., Joliet 60431

(815) 726-6161

Springfield State Journal-Register, 313 S. Sixth St., Springfield 62705,

(217) 544-5711

The Daily Journal, 362 S. Schmale Rd., Wheaton 60187

(312) 653-1000

Copley News Service syndicates more than 60 columns, some by staff members of its newspapers, and also by Phyllis Schlafly, Ralph deToledano and other non-staffers. Among the syndicated columnists are John Sinor and Neil Morgan, of the San Diego Tribune, and Don Freeman (TV), of the San Diego Union. Copley News Service has more than 2,000 clients.

Following is a list of the five regional bureaus of Copley News Service.

Los Angeles:
485A Hall of Administration, 500 W. Temple St., Los Angeles 90012
(213) 628-8927, Thom Mead

Sacramento:
1190 Park Executive Bldg., 925 L St., Sacramento 95814
(916) 443-4494, Robert Studer

San Diego:
350 Camino de la Reina, San Diego 92110
(714) 293-1824, Charles Ohi

Springfield:
Room 307, State Capitol, Springfield, Ill. 62706
(217) 544-3666, Ray Serati

Washington, D.C.:
1100 Ntl. Press Bldg., Wash., D.C. 20045
(202) 737-6960, L. Edgar Prina

SAN FRANCISCO

(The San Francisco Bay area includes The Tribune in Oakland, which is listed in the preceding section.)

RUNNER'S WORLD
Box 366, 1400 Stierlin Rd., Mountain View 94043
(415) 965-8777

Eastern:
72 Jefferson Ave., New London, CT 06320
(203) 447-2303, Amby Burfoot

6 E. 39 St., N.Y. 10016
(212) 889-9120, Stan Singer

SAN FRANCISCO CHRONICLE
901 Mission St., San Francisco 94119
(415) 777-1111

Oakland:
1330 Broadway, Oakland 94612
(415) 834-2880, Pearl Stewart, August Sairanen, Michael Taylor, George Williamson, Rob Haeseler

Redwood City:
466 St. Francis, Redwood City 94062
(415) 366-7787, Bill Workman

Sacramento:
>925 L St., Sacramento 95814
>
>(916) 445-5658, Gale Cook, Steve Wiegard, Ann Bancroft.

San Jose:
>Press Room, Civic Center, San Jose 95110
>
>(408) 998-0222, Rick Carroll

San Rafael:
>Marin County Court House, San Rafael 94902
>
>(415) 479-3377, Jack Viets

Washington, D.C.:
>5002 Jamestown Rd., Bethesda, Md. 20016
>
>(202) 484-8838, John Fogarty

Herb Caen, Stan Delaplane, Art Hoppe, and Terrance O'Flaherty are a few of the Chronicle columnists syndicated by Chronicle Features, San Francisco 94102. Charles McCabe died in 1983.

The San Francisco Chronicle is completely independent and does not share any bureaus with the San Francisco Examiner. The newspapers do share printing facilities and join in a Sunday newspaper, The San Francisco Examiner and Chronicle. The circulation of the morning Chronicle has increased to 530,000 and the circulation of the evening Examiner has remained about 158,000. The Sunday circulation is about 692,000. The Chronicle thus is the nation's 11th biggest daily.

SAN FRANCISCO EXAMINER
>Box 7260, 110 Fifth St., San Francisco 94120
>
>(415) 777-2424

East Bay:
>209A Oakland City Hall, 1421 Washington St., Oakland 94612
>
>(415) 834-8659, Charles Burress
>
>County Admin. Bldg., 1221 Oak St., Oakland 94612
>
>(415) 874-7955, Don Martinez,
>
>Box 628, Martinez 94533
>
>(415) 229-3655, Marguerite Hernandez

Marin:
>Press Rm., C—36, Hall of Justice, Civic Ctr., San Rafael 94903
>
>(415) 479-4114, John Todd

Peninsula:
>Press Rm., Hall of Justice, 401 Marshall St., Redwood City 94063
>
>(415) 365-7960, Don West, John Flinn, Leslie Guevarra
>
>177 Bovet Rd., San Mateo
>
>(415) 570-7281, Patricia Yollin, Stanton Samuelson

Sacramento:
>320-A Park Executive Bldg., 925 L St., Sacramento 95814
>
>(916) 445-4310, Gale Cook, Steve Capps

Washington, D.C.:
>   1701 Pennsylvania Ave., N.W., Wash., D.C. 20006
>   (202) 298-6920 Laurence McQuillan
>   (Hearst Newspapers)

TRAVELAGE WEST
>   Room 603, 582 Market St., San Francisco 94104
>   (415) 781-8353
>   This is the Western office of Official Airline Guides Travel Magazines,
which are headquartered in New York. The bureaus of all these publications
are listed under Travel Age.

SAN FRANCISCO BUREAUS (area code 415)

Advertising Age, 4119 Park Blvd., Palo Alto 94303, Stephen Beitler, 858-1247
American Banker, 235 Montgomery St., San Francisco 94104,
>   Geoff Brouillette, 362-1472
Associated Press, 318 Fox Plaza, San Francisco 94119, Martin C. Thompson,
>   621-7432
Aviation Week & Space Technology, 425 Battery St., San Francisco 94111,
>   Richard G. O'Lone, 362-4600
Business Week, 425 Battery St., San Francisco 94111,
>   Herbert Lawson, 362-4600
Byte, 425 Battery St., San Francisco 94133, Philip Temmons, 398-7990
Chemical & Engineering News, 1408 Shrader, San Francisco 94117,
>   Rudy Baum, 665-4971
Chemical Week, 425 Battery St., San Francisco 94111, Margaret Ralston
>   Drossel, Jenness Keene, 362-4600
Datamation, 2680 Bayshore Frontage Rd., Mountain View 94043, Ed Yasaki,
>   965-8222
Fairchild Publications, 760 Market St., San Francisco 94102, 781-8921
Industry Week, 1601 Bayshore Hwy., Burlingame 94010, William Patterson,
>   692-1381
Journal of Commerce, 110 Sutter St., San Francisco 94104, Maureen Robb,
>   433-3238
Los Angeles Times, 825 Fox Plaza, San Francisco 94102, 431-1600
McGraw-Hill World News Service, 425 Battery Street, San Francisco 94111,
>   Margaret Ralston Drossel, 362-4600
Medical World News, 40 Lansing St., San Francisco 94105, Judy Ismach,
>   777-3208
New York Times, 925 Fox Plaza Bldg., San Francisco 94102, Wallace Turner,
>   861-8662
Newsweek, 505 Sansone St., San Francisco 94111, Vern Smith, 788-2651
Official Airline Guides, 582 Market St., San Francisco 94104, Donald
>   Fangley, 781-8353

People, 100 Bush St., San Francisco 94104, Nancy Faber, 982-5000

Time, 100 Bush St., San Francisco 94104, Eileen Schields, 982-5000

Travel Weekly, 2203 Jones St., San Francisco 94133, Janet Felix, 885-6618

Travelage, 582 Market St., San Francisco 94104, 781-8353

US News & World Report, 601 California St., San Francisco 94108, Joanne Davidson, 781-2832

USA Today, 1390 Market St., San Francisco 94102, Lorrie Lynch, 861-3975

United Press International, 1212 Fox Plaza, Ninth & Market Sts., San Francisco 944102, 552-5900

Wall Street Journal, 220 Battery St., San Francisco 94119, Ken Slocum, 986-6886

SAN JOSE MERCURY NEWS

750 Ridder Park Dr., San Jose 95190

(408) 920-5456

The Mercury has a morning circulation of 165,000 and the News (evening 64,000) are combined on Saturday (217,000) and on Sunday (277,000).
Fremont:

37471 Fremont Blvd., Fremont 94536

(415) 791-1245, Sandi Dolbee

Monterey:

540 Arbrego St., Monterey 93940

(408) 372-6390, Mac Bowe

Peninsula:

2570 El Camino Real West, Mountain View 94040

(415) 941-4813, Patty Fisher

Sacramento:

925 L St., Sacramento 95814

(916) 441-4601, Dan Meyers

Santa Cruz:

1121 Pacific Ave., Santa Cruz 95060

(408) 423-3234, Jack Foley

South County:

Box 414, Gilroy 95020

(408) 847-1617, Bill Glines

Washington, D.C.:

1319 F St., N.W., Wash., D.C. 20004

(202) 637-3600, Robert S. Boyd (Knight-Ridder Newspapers)

COLORADO

THE DENVER POST

650 Fifteenth St., Denver 80202

(303) 820-1010

In 1982, the Post switched to morning publication, to enhance its competition with the Rocky Mountain News. Circulation of the Post is now (261,000 daily, 369,000 Sunday) vs. the Rocky Mountain News (261,000 daily, 285,000 Sunday). As is often the case, the Sunday dominance is achieved by increased distribution (and news coverage) beyond the metropolitan area and throughout the state.

Boulder:

> 1150 Hancock Dr., Boulder 80302
>
> (303) 433-4786, Jane Cracraft

Washington, D.C.:

> 245 Second St., S.E. Wash., D.C. 20003
>
> (202) 546-4464, Leonard Larsen

MULTICHANNEL NEWS

> 300 S. Jackson St., Denver 80209
>
> (303) 393-6397

A weekly tabloid started in late 1980 by Fairchild Publications. Unlike WWD and other Fairchild newspapers, this one is not headquartered in New York. Readers are in cable and pay TV.

Atlanta:

> 57 Executive Park South, N.E., Atlanta 30329
>
> (404) 633-8461, Ann Dukes

Los Angeles:

> 615 S. Flower St., L.A. 90017
>
> (213) 624-1981, Stewart Schley

New York:

> 633 Third Avenue, N.Y. 10017
>
> (212) 741-6208, Joe Butle

Washington, D.C.:

> 1333 H St., N.W., Wash., D.C., 29995
>
> (202) 682-3228, Lucy E. Hoffman

ROCKY MOUNTAIN NEWS

> 400 West Colfax, Denver 80204
>
> (303) 892-5000

Boulder:

> 3651 Pearl St., Boulder 80301
>
> (303) 442-8729, Chance Conner

Southern Colorado:

> 7 E. Bijou St., Colorado Springs 80903
>
> (303) 633-4442, Dick Foster

Fort Collins:

> 209 N. Commerce, Fort Collins 80524
>
> (303) 484-0620

Washington, D.C.:

    1110 Vermont Ave., N.W., Wash., D.C. 20005

    (202) 833-9250, Al Gordon

    (Scripps-Howard Newspaper Alliance. For additional information, see Cincinnati Post & Times-Star.)

SATELLITE COMMUNICATIONS

    6430 S. Yosemite St., Englewood 80111

    (303) 694-1522

New York:

    301 W. 53 St., N.Y. 10019

    (212) 246-7082, Jill Marks

Washington, D.C.:

    1900 L St., N.W., Wash., D.C. 20036

    (202) 659-0308, Art Hill

DENVER BUREAUS (area code 303)

Associated Press, 650 15th St., Denver 80202, Joe McGowan Jr., 825-0123

Business Week, 655 Broadway, Denver 80203, Sandra Atchison, 825-6731

Chicago Tribune, 11141 Vrain St., Westminster 80030, James Coates,
    322-3290

Fairchild Publications, 1762 Emerson St., Denver 80218, 832-4141

Los Angeles Times, 1415 Larimer St., Denver 80202, Bill Curry, 825-2345

New York Times, 2727 Bryant St., Denver 80211, William Schmidt,
    445-5570

Newsweek, 1420 Larimer St., Denver 80202, Jeff B. Copland, 592-1300

Pueblo Chieftain, Pueblo Star-Journal, 325 State Capitol Bldg., Denver
    81001, Tom McAvoy, 861-7202

Time, 2060 Dexter St., Denver 80207, Robert Wuimstodt,
    320-1141

U.S. News & World Report, 50 S. Steele St., Denver 80209,
    Gordon Witkin, 399-0160

United Press International, 720 S. Colorado Blvd., Denver
    80222, 758-2002

PUEBLO CHIEFTAIN
PUEBLO STAR-JOURNAL

Box 36, Pueblo 81002

(303) 544-3520

There are no weeklies in Pueblo and the morning Chieftain (circulation 39,000) and evening Star-Journal (circulation 14,500) cover the area south of Colorado Springs with an extensive bureau system.

Alamosa:

Box 923, Alamosa 81101

(303) 589-6161. Erin Smith (San Luis Valley Alamosa, Conejos, Costilla, Nineral, Rio Grande, Saguache counties)

Canon City:

1613 N. Seventh, Canon City 81212

(303) 275-4955, Caryl Buckstein (Fremont, Custer counties)

Denver:

Room 325, State Capitol Bldg., Denver 81001

(303) 861-7202, Tom McAvoy

Lamar:

801 S. 13th., Lamar 81052,

(303) 336-7383, Sue Binder (Baca, Kiowa, Prowers counties)

Leadville:

1841 Silver Eagle Dr., Leadville 80461

(303) 486-1179, Georgina Brown (Lake County)

Salida:

121 Wood, Salida 81201

(303) 539-3249, Dick Dixon (Chaffee County)

Swink:

Box 161, Swink 81077

(303) 384-7167, Loretta Scott (Otero, Crowley, Bent counties)

Trinidad:

155 E. Main, Trinidad 81082

(303) 846-4204, Tim McDonald (Huerfano, Las Animas counties)

Washington, D.C.:

123 Sixth St., S.E., Wash., D.C. 20003

(202) 546-1350, Helene Monberg

CONNECTICUT

UNITED STATES BANKER
1 River Rd., Cos Cob 06807
(203) 661-5000
Boston:
Box 2386, Woburn 01888
(617) 938-9009, John Clark
Washington, D.C.:
5927 Merritt Pl., Falls Church, VA 22041
(703) 931-1988, Raoul Edwards

McNAUGHT SYNDICATE
537 Steamboat Rd., Greenwich 06830
(203) 661-4990
One of the nation's oldest syndicates, McNaught distributes Joe Palooka and other comics, as well as columns by the following:
John Keasler, Miami News, Miami, FL 33101
Andrew Tully, 2104 48 St., N.W., Wash., D.C. 20007

THE HARTFORD COURANT
285 Broad St., Hartford 06115
(203) 241-6200
With a morning circulation of 214,000 and a Sunday circulation of 281,000, the Courant has a considerably larger circulation than any other Connecticut newspaper. Established in 1764, The Hartford Courant (America's oldest newspaper of continuous publication) covers central Connecticut. The Courant was purchased by the Times Mirror Co. in 1979. The Courant has eight bureaus in the state, a Washington bureau and a Boston bureau, which was recently opened.
All Connecticut bureaus have area code 203.
Enfield:
810 Enfield St., Enfield 06082
741-2156, Joseph P. Burns
Groton:
8 School St., Groton 06340
445-8121, Michael Golay
Manchester:
71 E. Center St., Manchester 06040
649-8601, Jeffrey R. Kotkin
Middletown:
Plaza Middlesex, 300 Main St., Middletown 06457
346-4473, Peter B. Pach

New Britain:
>100 E. Main St., New Britain 06050
>229-6155, Karen Bailey

New Haven:
>152 Temple St., New Haven 06510
>777-3676, Kristi Vaughan

Stamford:
>1351 Washington Blvd., Stamford 06902
>964-0879, Michele Block

West Hartford:
>41 S. Main St., West Hartford 06107
>521-9442, Carol Fry

Boston:
>184 High St., Boston 02110
>(617) 679-6299, Bruce DeSilva

Washington, D.C.:
>1730 Rhode Island Ave., N.W., Wash., D.C. 20036
>(202) 822-8040, Bill Stall

THE NEW HAVEN REGISTER
THE JOURNAL-COURIER

>Long Wharf, 40 Sargent Dr., New Haven 06511
>(203) 562-1121

The Journal-Courier, a morning newspaper, was founded in 1755. The New Haven Register, a major evening newspaper in southern Connecticut, was established in 1812. The 1983 circulation of the Journal-Courier was 39,000. 1983 circulation of the Register was 92,000 daily and 137,000 Sundays. They jointly have an extensive bureau system. (The Connecticut area code is 203.)

Ansonia:
>262 Main St., Ansonia 06401
>734-2813, Don Anderson

Hartford:
>State Capitol Bldg., Hartford 06115
>566-4566, James Mutrie

Madison:
>724 Boston Post Rd., Madison 06443
>245-7325, Jack Kramer

Milford:
>58 River St., Milford 06460
>877-5168, Paul Jackson

Old Saybrook:
>806 Boston Post Rd., Old Saybrook 06457
>388-4428, Jack Kramer

Wallingford:
>50 S. Main St., Wallingford 06492
>269-1496, James Fleming

GOLF DIGEST
TENNIS
>Box 5350, 495 Westport Ave., Norwalk 06856
>(203) 847-5811
>These two major magazines are published by the New York Times Magazine Group. No bureaus.

ON CABLE MAGAZINE
>Box 239, Norwalk 06856
>(203) 866-6256
>No bureaus.

PROGRESSIVE GROCER
>1351 Washington Blvd., Stamford 06902
>(203) 325-3500
>This major trade publication moved in 1983 from New York to Connecticut. Lynn Densford of the Washington bureau receives her mail via the Connecticut office.

DELAWARE

WILMINGTON EVENING JOURNAL
WILMINGTON MORNING NEWS
>Box 1111, 831 Orange St., Wilmington 19899
>(302) 573-2000, (800) 235-9100
>There are only three daily newspapers in Delaware—fewer than in any other state—and two of them, the Wilmington Evening Journal (64,000) and Wilmington Morning News (64,000), are published by the same company, which is part of the Gannett Co. The other daily is the Delaware State News (26,000) in Dover.
>On Sundays, the state has the Sunday News Journal (125,000) and Delaware State News (30,000). The bureaus of the News-Journal papers, under the direction of Isabel Spencer, cover the entire state of Delaware.

Dover:
>20 E. Division St., Dover 19901
>(302) 734-7577
>(Dover, Kent county and portions of Eastern shore of Maryland)

Sussex:
>18 N. Railroad Ave., Georgetown 19947
>(302) 856-7371
>(Sussex county and portions of Eastern shore of Maryland)

Newark:

> 62 N. Chapel St., Newark 19711
>
> (302) 738-6000, Alan Mueller
>
> (Newark area; Cecil county, Md., and Southeast Pa.)

Washington, D.C.:

> 1000 Wilson Blvd., Arlington, VA 22209
>
> (703) 276-5800 (Gannett)

DISTRICT OF COLUMBIA

ARMY TIMES PUBLISHING CO.

> 475 School St., S.W., Wash., D.C. 20024
>
> (202) 554-7278
>
> Four weekly tabloid newspapers, Air Force Times (138,000), Army

Times (142,000), Navy Times (97,000) and Federal Times (51,000) are operated with a battery of correspondents. Three editions (U.S., European and Pacific) are printed of each of the three military publications. All news is channeled through the main office.

BROADCASTING

> 1735 De Sales St., N.W., Wash., D.C. 20036
>
> (202) 638-1022

Los Angeles:

> 1680 N. Vine St., Hollywood 90028
>
> (213) 463-3148, Richard Mahler

New York:

> 630 Third Ave., N.Y. 10017
>
> (212) 599-2830, Kathy Haley
>
> These two bureaus are in the network centers and are quite active as

''The newsweekly of broadcasting and allied arts.''

CHEMICAL & ENGINEERING NEWS

> 1155 Sixteenth Street, N.W., Wash., D.C. 20036
>
> (202) 872-4600

Chicago:

> 176 W. Adams St., Chicago 60603
>
> (312) 236-7325, Ward Worthy

Houston:

> Box 27620, Houston 77027
>
> (713) 522-4125, Bruce Greek

New York:

> 405 Lexington Ave., N.Y. 10017
>
> (212) 697-3223, William Storck

San Francisco:
>1408 Shrader, San Francisco 94117
>(415) 665-4971, Rudy Baum
>Copies of news releases also should be sent to the main office of
this weekly magazine, which is published by the American Chemical Society.

GANNETT NEWS SERVICE
>1627 K St., N.W., Wash., D.C. 20006
>(202) 862-4900, John Curley
>This large operation, with bureaus in California, Florida, Michigan,
New Jersey and New York, is described under Rochester, N.Y., which is headquarters of the Gannett Company.

HEARST NEWSPAPERS
>1701 Pennsylvania Ave., N.W., Wash., D.C. 20006
>(202) 298-6920, Joseph Kingsbury Smith, national editor and columnist
>This is the only Hearst bureau. It was expanded in late 1978. For fur-
ther information, see the listing about Hearst in the New York City section.

MEDILL NEWS SERVICE
>806 15 St., N.W., Wash., D.C. 20005
>(202) 347-8700
>This operation is part of the graduate program of the Medill School of
Journalism, Northwestern University. Graduate students work, for an
academic quarter, as correspondents for several radio stations and the following newspapers:
>>Anderson (SC) Independent-Mail
>>Beaver County (PA) Times
>>Biloxi (MS) Herald and Sun
>>Bismarck (ND) Tribune
>>Chicago (IL) Lerner Home Newspapers
>>Great Falls (MT) Tribune
>>Green Bay (WI) Press-Gazette
>>Lawrence (MA) Eagle-Tribune
>>Livingston (MT) Enterprise
>>Miles City (MT) Star
>>Mankato (MN) The Land
>>Oak Ridge (TN) Oak Ridger
>>Ogden (UT) Standard-Examiner
>>Rapid City (SD) Journal
>>Sulphur Springs (TX) Country World

NATIONAL GEOGRAPHIC
>Seventeenth and M Sts., Wash., D.C. 20036
>(202) 857-7000

With a circulation of more than 10 million, this monthly magazine is extremely important and well known throughout the world. Paul Simpson is chief of the National Geographic News Service.

NEWHOUSE NEWS SERVICE

1750 Pennsylvania Ave., Wash., D.C. 20006

(202) 383-7800

The Newhouse Newspapers include 29 newspapers from coast-to-coast. The Newhouse News Service, headed by Robert G. Fichenberg in Washington, D.C., services all of the newspapers, as well as over 125 sub-scribers. Distribution is via Independent Press Service (formerly Field News Service). The Birmingham News, New Orleans Times-Picayune/States Item, The Star-Ledger (Newark, N.J.), and St. Louis Globe-Democrat are listed sepa-rately. The Washington correspondents of other Newhouse newspapers include Mike Rood, who covers for The Patriot and The Evening News in Harrisburg, Pa.; Randy Quarles who covers for The Huntsville Times, The Mobile Press and The Mobile Register in Alabama, and the Mississippi Press in Pascagoula; Terry Kivlan, who covers for the Staten Island Advance in N.Y.C., Syracuse Herald-Journal and The Post-Standard in Syracuse, N.Y.; Miranda Spivack, who covers for The Springfield Daily News in Springfield, Mass., and Robert D.G. Lewis, who is chief correspondent for the 8 Booth newspapers of Michigan.

Love Miller Jr. writes a weekly column, The Presidency. Otis Pike writes a semi-weekly column of political commentary.

TELEVISION DIGEST

1836 Jefferson Pl., N.W., Wash., D.C. 20036

(202) 872-9200

New York:

475 Fifth Ave., N.Y. 10017

(212) 686-5410, Dave Lachenbruch.

U.S. NEWS & WORLD REPORT

2300 N St., N.W., Wash., D.C. 20037

(202) 861-2240

Circulation of this weekly news magazine is 2,050,000. A bureau recently was opened in Denver. Don Battle is chief of domestic bureaus.

Atlanta:

2308 Peachtree Center, So. Tower, 225 Peachtree St., S.E.,

Atlanta 30303

(404) 688-1331, Linda Lanier

Chicago:

1433 Tribune Sq., 435 N. Michigan Ave., Chicago 60611

(312) 329-0890, Michael Bose, Mary Galligan

Denver:
> 50 S. Steele, Denver 80209
> (303) 399-0160, Gordon Witkin

Detroit:
> 1120 Free Press Bldg., 321 W. Lafayette St., Detroit 48226
> (313) 963-6757, Jack Seamonds, Carey English

Houston:
> 1965 Texas Commerce Tower, Houston 77002
> (713) 227-6163, Joseph Benham; Sarah Peterson (Bureau Chief)

Los Angeles:
> 9465 Wilshire Blvd., Beverly Hills 90212
> (213) 274-9404, Juanita R. Hogue; Joseph Galloway

New York:
> 45 Rockefeller Plaza, N.Y. 10020
> (212) 246-3366, Ron Scherer

San Francisco:
> Suite 204, 601 California, San Francisco 94108
> (415) 781-2832, Joanne Davidson

Washington, D.C.:
> 2300 N. St., N.W., Wash., D.C. 20037
> (202) 861-2368, Warner Ragsdale, Jr.

USA TODAY

> Box 500, Wash., D.C. 20044
> (703) 276-3400

USA Today is located in its own new building at 1000 Wilson Blvd., Arlington, VA 22209. Started in 1982 by Gannett, the colorful newspaper is distributed five days a week (Monday to Friday) throughout the country. Its 1983 circulation was over a million.

USA Today uses the Gannett bureaus, as well as its own bureaus:

Atlanta:
> Box 77053, Atlanta 30357
> (404) 892-1611, John Head

Chicago:
> 6 N. Michigan Ave., Chicago 60602
> (312) 263-2591, Steve Wilson

Houston:
> 708 Main St., Houston 77002
> (713) 223-5688, Julie Morris

Los Angeles:
> 924 Westwood Blvd., Los Angeles 90024
> (213) 208-6425, Eric Brazil

Minneapolis:
> 1200 Nichollet Mall, Minneapolis 55403
> (612) 338-1173, Tim Schreiner

New York:
>535 Madison Ave., N.Y. 10022
>
>(212) 715-5410, Joel Dreyfuss

Pittsburgh:
>1000 RIDC Plaza, Pittsburgh 15238
>
>(412) 963-0808

San Francisco:
>1390 Market St., San Francisco 94102
>
>(415) 861-3975, Lorrie Lynch

THE WASHINGTON POST

>1150 15 St. N.W., Wash., D.C. 20071
>
>(202) 334-6000

Atlanta:
>Suite 1210, 229 Peachtree St., Atlanta 30303
>
>(404) 586-9650

Austin:
>Suite 645, Littlefield Bldg., Austin 78701
>
>(512) 473-2291

Chicago:
>Room 519A, 401 N. Wabash Ave., Chicago 60611
>
>(312) 321-3000

Los Angeles:
>Suite 378, 10100 Santa Monica Blvd., Century City 90067
>
>(213) 277-4819

Miami:
>514 Palermo, Coral Gables 33134
>
>(305) 446-6872

New York:
>444 Madison Ave., N.Y. 10022
>
>(212) 350-2588

Maryland bureaus are located in Baltimore, Annapolis and Montgomery and Prince George counties. Virginia bureaus are in Richmond, Alexandria and Arlington and Fairfax counties. Correspondence to these bureaus generally is channeled through Bill McAllister, Virginia editor; Don Baker, Maryland editor; Claudia Townsend, District editor; or Larry Kramer, Metropolitan editor. Separate weekly sections are published on Thursday, called the Virginia Weekly, the Maryland Weekly and the District Weekly.

Daily circulation in 1983 was an all-time high of 718,000 and Sunday circulation was 997,000 (fifth biggest).

New bureaus recently were opened in Austin and Miami.

The Washington Post is one of the largest circulation and most influential newspapers in the country. It also operates the Eastern half of the Los Angeles Times-Washington Post news service, which is distributed to major newspapers.

Post staffers whose columns are syndicated include David S. Broder (politics), Herbert L. Block (Herblock cartoons), Hobart Rowen (economics), Lou Cannon (commentary), William Raspberry (commentary), Colman McCarthy (commentary) and Tom Shales (television columnist).

WASHINGTON TIMES

3600 New York Ave., N.W., Wash., D.C. 20002
(202) 636-3305
No bureaus.

WASHINGTON BUREAUS (area code 202)

Abilene Reporter-News, 292 Ntl. Press Bldg., Wash., D.C. 20045, Bill Garland, Phil Swann, 628-1585

Advertising Age, Ntl. Press Bldg., Wash., D.C. 20045, Richard L. Gordon, 662-7200

Akron Beacon Journal, 1319 F St., N.W., Wash., D.C. 20004, David Hess, 637-3600

Albany Times-Union, Knickerbocker News, 1701 Pennsylvania Ave., N.W., Wash., D.C. 20006, Joseph Kingsbury Smith, 298-6920

Albuquerque Journal, 3267 P St., N.W., Wash., D.C. 20007, Paul Wieck, 338-2240

Albuquerque Tribune, 1110 Vermont Ave., N.W., D.C. 20005, Jerry Conto, 347-7750

Allentown Call-Chronicle, 316 Pennsylvania Ave., S.E., Wash., D.C. 20003, 546-7500

Amarillo Globe News, Suite 409, 236 Massachusetts Ave., N.E., Wash., D.C. 20002

American Banker, 1180 Ntl. Press Bldg., Wash., D.C. 20045, Robert Trigoux, 347-5529

American Medical News, 1101 Vermont Ave., N.W., Wash., D.C. 20005, Sharon McIlrath, 789-7400

Anchorage Daily News, 203 C St., N.E., Wash., D.C. 20002, Karin Davies, 547-4077

Arizona Republic, 641 Ntl. Press Bldg., Wash., D.C. 20045, Benjamin R. Cole, 638-6425

Arkansas Gazette, 605 14th St., N.W., Wash., D.C. 20004, Carol Mattack, 347-9403

Associated Press, 2021 K St., N.W., Wash., D.C. 20006, Walter Mears, 833-5300

Atlanta Constitution, Atlanta Journal, 1901 Pennsylvania Ave., N.W., Wash., D.C. 20006, 331-0900

Atlantic City Press, 316 Pennsylvania Ave., S.E., Wash., D.C. 20003, 546-7500

Austin American Statesman, 1901 Pennsylvania Ave., N.W., Wash., D.C. 20006, Linda Simon, 331-0900

Automotive News, 515 Ntl. Press Bldg., Wash., D.C. 20045, Helen Kahn, 638-5300

Aviation Week & Space Technology, 1777 N Kent St., Arlington, VA 22209, Herbert Coleman, William Gregory, (202) 463-1770

Baltimore News-American, 1701 Pennsylvania Ave., N.W., Wash., D.C. 20006, Joseph Kingsbury Smith, 298-6920

Baltimore Sun, 1627 K St., N.W., Wash., D.C. 20006, Ernest Ferguson Jr., 347-8250

Bangor Daily News, 1220 Maryland Ave., N.E., Wash., D.C. 20002, John S. Day, 398-5637

Battle Creek Enquirer, 1000 Wilson Blvd., Arlington, VA 22209, James Geehan, (703) 276-5800

Bergen Record, 987 Ntl. Press Bldg., Wash., D.C. 20045, Robert Cunningham, 638-2127

Billboard, 733 15th St., N.W., Wash., D.C. 20005, Bill Holland, 783-3282

Birmingham News, 1750 Pennsylvania Ave., N.W., Wash., D.C. 20005, Gayle McCracken, 833-9520

Bond Buyer, 529 Fourteenth St., N.W., Wash., D.C. 20045, Craig Ferris, 293-4727

Boston Globe, 1750 Pennsylvania Ave., N.W., Washington, D.C. 20006, 393-6020

Boston Herald, 533 National Bldg., Wash., D.C. 20045, Niles Lathen, 313-1531

Buffalo News, 12284 Ntl. Press Bldg., Wash., D.C. 20045, Richard D. McCarthy, 737-3188

Business Insurance, 1253 Ntl. Press Bldg., Wash., D.C. 20045, Jerry Geisel, 638-5300

Business Marketing, 1253 Ntl. Press Bldg., Wash., D.C. 20045, Rick Gordon, 638-5300

Business Week, 400 Ntl. Press Bldg., Wash., D.C. 20045, Robert E. Farrell, 737-6630

Cahners Publishing Company, 968 Ntl. Press Bdg., Wash., D.C. 20045, David Heinly, 626-2772

Camden Courier-Post, Box 500, Wash., D.C. 20044, 267-5800

Cash Box, 3518 N. Utah St., Arlington, VA 22207, Earl B. Abrams, (703) 243-5664

Chain Store Age, 177-35 Striley Dr., Wash., D.C. 20861, Kenneth Rankin, 774-3895

Charlotte News and Observer, 1319 F St., N.W., Wash., D.C. 20004, Steve Kelly, 637-3628

Charlotte Observer, 1319 F St., N.W., Wash., D.C. 20004, Bill Arthur, 627-3600

Chemical Week, 1120 Vermont Ave., N.W., Wash., D.C. 20045, Robert E. Farrell, 463-1600

Chicago Sun-Times, 708 Ntl. Press Bldg., Wash., D.C. 20045, Patrick Oster, 785-8200

Chicago Tribune, 1707 H Street, N.W., Wash., D.C. 20006, Raymond Coffey, 785-9430

Christian Science Monitor, 910 16th St., N.W., Wash., D.C. 20006, Charlotte Saikowski, 785-4400

Cincinnati Enquirer, Box 7858, Wash., D.C. 20044, 276-5800

Cincinnati Post, 1110 Vermont Ave., N.W., Wash., D.C. 20005, Jerry Condo, 833-9250

Cleveland Plain Dealer, 521 Ntl. Press Building, Wash., D.C. 20045, Thomas Brazaitis, 638-1366

Columbia Record, 6817 Old Stage Rd., Rockville, MD 20852, Yeland Banoly, (301) 881-2220

Columbus Citizen-Journal, 1110 Vermont Ave., N.W., Wash., D.C. 20005, Jerry Condo, 833-9250

Columbus Dispatch, 809 Ntl. Press Building, Wash., D.C. 20045, George Embrey, 347-3144.

Computerworld, 821 Ntl. Press Bldg., Wash., D.C. 20045, Jake Kirchner, 347-6718

Corpus Christi Caller-Times, 292 Ntl. Press Bldg., Wash., D.C. 20045, Bill Garland, 628-1585

Daily Oklahoman, Oklahoma City Times, 907 Ntl. Press Bldg., Wash., D.C. 20045, Allan W. Cromley, 628-0335

Dallas Morning News, 295 Ntl. Press Bldg., Wash., D.C. 20045, Carl Yeubsdorf,737-6127

Dallas Times-Herald, 559 Ntl. Press Bldg., Wash., D.C. 20045, Paul West, 638-0404

Dayton Daily News, 1901 Pennsylvania Ave., N.W., Wash., D.C. 20006, Tom Price, 331-0900

Denver Post, 245 Second St., S.E., Wash., D.C. 20003, Leonard Laisen, 546-4464

Des Moines Register, 1317 F St., N.W., Wash., D.C. 20004, James Risser, 347-9111

Detroit Free Press, 1195 Ntl. Press Bldg., Wash., D.C. 20045, Bob Boyd, 637-3600

Detroit News, 425 Ntl. Press Bldg., Wash., D.C. 20045, Gary Schuster, 628-4566

Donrey Media Group, 1068 Ntl. Press Bldg., Wash., D.C. 20045, Eric Ruff, 787-1760

Dun's Business Month, 912 S 26 Pl., Arlington, VA 22202, Marilyn Wilson, (703) 549-0881

Editor & Publisher, 1295 Ntl. Press Bldg., Wash., D.C. 20045, James E. Roher, 628-8365

El Paso Times, 1627 K St., N.W., Wash., D.C. 20006, 862-4900

Electronics, 433 Ntl. Press Bldg., Wash., D.C. 20045, Ray Connolly, Karen Beiney, 462-1650

Esquire, 3748 Huntington St., N.W., Wash., D.C. 20015, Jerrold Schecter, 362-9040

Eugene Register-Guard, 210 Seventh St., S.E., Wash., D.C. 20003, Steve Forrester, 543-1878

Fairchild Publications, 1333 H. St., N.W., Wash., D.C. 20045, Lloyd Schwartz, 682-3200

Forbes, 399 Ntl. Press Bldg., Wash., D.C. 20045, Jerry Flint, 628-2344

Fort Lauderdale News & Sun-Sentinel, Suite 910, 1707 H. St., N.W., Wash., D.C. 20006, William Gibson, 293-9037

Fort Worth Star-Telegram, 1096 Ntl. Press Building, Wash., D.C. 20045, Dave Montgomery, 638-3107

Fortune, 919 18 St., N.W., Wash., D.C. 20006, Paul Weaver, 429-9620

Fresno Bee, 203 C St., N.E., Wash., D.C. 20002, Leo Rennert, John Johnson, Jeff Raimundo, 547-4044

Gannett Co., 1000 Wilson Blvd., Arlington, VA 22209, Robert Dueill, (703) 276-5800

Gannett News Service, 1627 K St., N.W., Wash., D.C. 20006, John Curley, 862-4900

Gary Post-Tribune, 1319 F St., N.W., Wash., D.C. 20044, Charlie Green, 637-3600

Grand Forks Herald, 1319 F St., N.W., Wash., D.C. 20004, Jim McGregor, 637-3600

Grand Rapids Press, 1750 Pennsylvania Ave., N.W., Wash., D.C., Robert Fichenberg, 383-7800

Green Bay Press-Gazette, 1000 Wilson Blvd., Arlington, VA 22209, Robert Dubill, (703) 276-5800

Harrisburg Patriot/Evening News, 1750 Pennsylvania Ave., N.W., Wash., D.C., 20006, Robert Frichenberg, 383-7800

Hartford Courant, 1730 Rhode Island Ave., N.W., Wash., D.C. 20036, Bill Stall, 822-8040

Hearst Corporation, 1701 Pennsylvania Ave., N.W., Wash., D.C. 20006, Joseph Kingsbury Smith, 298-6920

Hollywood Reporter, 1234 Ntl. Press Bldg., Wash., D.C. 20045, Theresa McMasters, 737-2828

Hollywood Sun-Tattler, 777 14 St., N.W., Wash., D.C. 20005, B. J. Cutter, 347-7750

Honolulu Star-Bulletin, Box 7858, Wash., D.C. 20044, Dave Shapiro, (703) 276-5811

Houston Chronicle, 1750 Pennsylvania Ave., N.W., Wash., D.C. 20006, Cragg Hines, 429-1990

Houston Post, 291 Ntl. Press Bldg., Wash., D.C. 20045, Jim Craig, 638-4332

Idaho Statesman, 1000 Wilson Blvd., Arlington, VA, 22209, Jim Geehan, (703) 276-5800

Indianapolis News, 641 Ntl. Press Bldg., Wash., D.C. 20045, Benjamin R. Cole, 638-6425

Industry Week, 1030 15 St., N.W., Wash., D.C. 20005, John S. McClenahen, William H. Miller, 223-6650

Jet, 1750 Pennsylvania Ave., N.W., Wash., D.C. 20006, Simeon Booker, 393-5860

Journal of Commerce, Rm. 300, 1319 F St., N. W., Wash., D.C. 20004, Tom Connors, 637-3670

Kansas City Star, 1319 F St., N.W., Wash., D.C. 20004, Andrew Miller, 393-2020

Lincoln Journal, 3850 Tanlaw Rd., N.W., #212, Wash., D.C. 20007, David E. Lynch, 244-0241

Long Beach Press-Telegram, 1319 F St., N.W., Wash., D.C. 20004, Carl Cammon, 637-3621

Los Angeles Herald Examiner, 1701 Pennsylvania Ave., N.W., Wash., D.C. 20006, Joseph Kingsbury Smith, 298-6920

Los Angeles Times, 1875 Eye St., N.W., Wash., D.C. 20006, Jack Nelson, 293-4650

Louisville Courier Journal, 986 Ntl. Press Bldg., Wash., D.C. 20045, Mike Brown, 628-7704

McGraw-Hill World News Service, 1120 Vermont Ave., N.W., Wash., D.C. 20045, Robert E. Farrell, 463-1600

McNaught Syndicate, 2104 48th St., N.W., Wash., D.C. 20007, Andrew Tully

Medical Economics, Suite 902, 200 N Globe Rd., Arlington, VA 22203, Karen Hunt, (703) 243-8082

Medical World News, Box 53414, Wash., D.C. 20009, Don Gibbons, Fran Pollner, 737-1078

Memphis Commercial Appeal, 1110 Vermont Ave., N.W., Wash., D.C. 20005, Morris Cunningham, Mary Oeihel, 347-7750

Miami Herald, 1319 F St., N.W., Wash., D.C. 20004, Robert Shaw Jr., 637-3600

Milwaukee Journal, 259 Ntl. Press Bldg., Wash., D.C. 20045, John W. Kole, 737-2985

Milwaukee Sentinel, 1290 Ntl. Press Bldg., Wash., D.C. 20045, Richard Bradee, 628-8920

Minneapolis Star & Tribune, 131 F St., N.W., Wash., D.C. 20004, Finlay Lewis, 347-5885

Multichannel News, 1333 H. St., N.W., Wash., D.C. 20005, Lucy E. Hoffman, 682-3228

New Hampshire Union Leader, 13514 Duhart Rd., Germantown, MD 20874, Thomas Gorey, (301) 972-4140

New Orleans Times-Picayune/States-Item, 1029 Ntl. Press Bldg., Wash., D.C. 20045, Edgar Poe, 383-7824.

New York Post, 1333H. St., N.W., Wash., D.C. 20005, 393-1531

New York Times, 1000 Connecticut Ave., N.W., Wash., D.C. 20036, Ben Franklin, 862-0300

Newark Star-Ledger, 1750 Pennsylvania Ave., Wash., D.C. 20006, Robert Cohen, 383-7823

Newsday, 1301 Pennsylvania Ave., Wash., D.C. 20006, 393-5630

Newsweek, 1750 Pennsylvania Ave., N.W., Wash., D.C. 20006, Mel Elfin, 626-2000

Official Airline Guides, 1625 Eye St., Wash., D.C. 20006, Barbara Cook, 659-4525

Omaha World-Herald, 895 Ntl. Press Bldg., Wash., D.C. 20045, Darwin R. Olofson, 393-0644

Oregon Journal, 1750 Pennsylvania Ave., N.W., Wash., D.C. 20006, Joseph Berger, 298-7080

Oregonian, 1750 Pennsylvania Ave., N.W., Wash., D.C. 20006, David Whitney, Jim Flanigan, 383-7825

Orlando Sentinel, Suite 910, 1707 H St., N.W., Wash., D.C. 20006, Anne Groer, 293-6885

Palm Beach Post, 1901 Pennsylvania Ave., N.W., Wash., D.C. 20006, Andy Glass, 331-0900

People, 888 16 St., N.W., Wash., D.C. 20006, Garry Clifford, 293-4300

Philadelphia Inquirer, 1319 F St., N.W., Wash., D.C. 20004, Michael Hobbs, 637-3600

Phoenix Gazette, 641 Ntl. Press Bldg., Wash., D.C. 20045, Sean Griffin, 638-6425

Pittsburgh Post-Gazette, 1280 Ntl. Press Bldg., Wash., D.C. 20045, Jane Boltzer, 393-4580

Pittsburgh Press, 1110 Vermont Ave., N.W., Wash., D.C. 20005, Kathy Kiely, 833-9250

Providence Journal, 728 Ntl. Press Bldg., Wash., D.C. 20045, John Mulligan, 628-6214

Pueblo Chieftain, Pueblo Star-Journal, 123 Sixth St., S.E., Wash., D.C. 20003, Helene Monberg, 546-1350

Restaurants & Institutions, Suite 639, 1435 G St., N.W., Wash., D.C. 20005, Sylvia Riggs, 628-2773

Riverside Press-Enterprise, 14 Tenth St., Wash., D.C. 20002, Martin
Salditch, 546-1914

Rochester Democrat & Chronicle/Rochester Times-Union, 1627 K St.,
Wash., D.C. 20006, James Guhan, 862-4500

Rocky Mountain News, 1110 Vermont Ave., N.W., Wash., D.C. 20005, Al
Gordon, 833-9250

Sacramento Bee, 203 C St., N.E., Wash., D.C. 20002, Leo Rennert,
574-4044

Salt Lake City Deseret News, 1502 Stonewall Rd., Alexandria, VA 22302
Gordon E. White, (703) 683-4019

Salt Lake City Tribune, 13514 Duhart Rd., Germantown, MD,
(301) 972-4140, Tom Gorey

San Antonio Express, San Antonio News, 533 Ntl. Press Building, Wash.,
D.C. 20045, Niles Yathem, 313-1531

San Antonio Light, 510 First Ntl. Bank Bldg., 1701 Pennsylvania Ave., N.W.,
Wash., D.C. 20006, 298-6920

San Diego Tribune, 1100 Ntl. Press Bldg., Wash., D.C. 20045, George
Condan, 737-6960

San Diego Union, 1100 Ntl. Press Bldg., Wash., D.C. 20045, L. Edgar
Prina, 737-6960

San Francisco Chronicle, 5002 Jamestown Rd., Bethesda, MD 20016, John
Fogarty, 484-8838

San Jose Mercury News, 1319 F St., N.W., Wash., D.C. 20004, Robert S.
Boyd, 637-3600

Satellite Communications, 1900 L St., N.W., Wash., D.C. 20036, Art Hill,
659-0308

Seattle Post-Intelligencer, 510 First National Bank Bldg., 1701 Pennsylvania
Ave., N.W., Wash., D.C. 20006, Joseph Kingsbury Smith, 298-6920

Seattle Times, 318 6 St., N.E., Wash., D.C. 20002, Ross Anderson,
543-4386

Shreveport Times, Box 7858, Wash., D.C. 20044, Mike Meacham,
276-5800

Sioux Falls Argus-Leader, 1627 K St., N.W., Wash., D.C. 20006, John J.
Curley, 862-4900

Sports Illustrated, 1333 H St., N.W., Wash., D.C. 20005, Norma Tangley,
371-1787

St. Louis Globe-Democrat, Suite 1320, 1750 Pennsylvania Ave., N.W., Wash.,
D.C. 20006, Edward W. O'Brien, 383-7846

St. Louis Post-Dispatch, 1701 Pennsylvania Ave., N.W., Wash., D.C. 20006,
298-6880

St. Paul Dispatch/Pioneer Press, 1319 F St., N.W., Wash., D.C. 20004, Steve
Dornfeld, 637-3600

St. Petersburg Times, 1414-22nd St., N.W., Wash., D.C. 20037, Charles
Stafford, 296-8583

TV Guide, 818 18th St., N.W., Wash., D.C. 20006, John Weisman, 822-8632

Tallahassee Democrat, 1319 F St., N.W., Wash., D.C. 20004, Jon Peterson, 637-3600

Tampa Tribune, 214 Ntl. Press Bldg., Wash., D.C. 20045, John Hall, 347-7770

Television/Radio Age, 716 W. Wayne St., Arlington, VA 22204, Howard Fields, (703) 521-4187

Time, 888 16th St., N.W., Wash., D.C. 20006, Robert Ajemiani, 293-4300

Toledo Blade, 1280 Ntl. Press Bldg., Wash., D.C. 20045, Roland Powell, 393-4580

Topeka Capitol-Journal, 605 14th St., N.W., Wash., D.C. 20014, Ken Peterson, 783-3274

Travel Trade, 3611 39th St., N.W., Wash., D.C. 20016, Don Knoles, 363-7316

Travel Weekly, 1156 15th St., N.W, Wash., D.C. 20005, Fran Durbin, 293-3400

Travelage East/Travelage Southeast/Travel Management Daily/Travel Management Newsletter, 1625 Eye St., N.W., Wash., D.C. 20006, Barbara Cook, 659-4525

Trentonian, 654 Pennsylvania Ave., N.E., Wash., D.C. 20003, John Membrino, 546-9876

Tulsa Daily World, 1278 Ntl. Press Bldg., Wash., D.C. 20045, Malvina Stephenson, 347-8557

USA Today, Box 500, Wash., D.C. 20044, 276-3400

United Press, 1400 I St., Wash., D.C. 20005, 289-0909

United States Banker, 5927 Merritt Pl., Falls Church, VA 22041, Raoul Edwards, (703) 931-1988

Variety, 1483 Chain Bridge Rd., McLean, VA 22101, Paul Harris, (703) 448-0510

Wall Street Journal, 1025 Connecticut Ave., Wash., D.C. 20036, Al Hunt, 862-9200

Wheaton Journal, 1100 Ntl. Press Bldg., Wash., D.C. 20045, L. Edgar Prina, 737-6960

Wichita Eagle-Beacon, 1319 F St., N.W., Wash., D.C. 20004, Robert S. Boyd, 637-3600

Wilmington Evening Journal, 1000 Wilson Blvd., Arlington, VA 22209, (703) 276-5800

Winston-Salem Journal, 214 Ntl. Press Bldg., Wash., D.C. 20045, Gene Marlowe, 347-7770

Worcester Telegram, 1237 Ntl. Press Bldg., Wash., D.C. 20045, Betty Mills, 554-3579

FLORIDA

FORT LAUDERDALE NEWS AND SUN-SENTINEL

Box 14430, 101 N. New River Dr., East, Ft. Lauderdale 33302

(305) 761-4000

The morning Sun-Sentinel has a circulation of 83,000 and the evening News has a circulation of 97,000. On weekends, when they combine as the News and Sun-Sentinel, the Saturday circulation is 176,000 and the Sunday circulation is 222,000.

Boca Raton:

3521 N. Federal Hwy., Boca Raton 33431

(305) 395-5950, Jeff Rodack (Mr. Rodack also supervises the Lake Worth office, as both are in Palm Beach County).

Hollywood:

4506 Hollywood Blvd., Hollywood 33021

(305) 966-4039, Ken Kaye

Lake Worth:

2324 S. Congress Ave., W. Palm Beach 33406

(305) 439-5000, Jeff Rodack

Lauderdale Lakes:

4000 N. State Rd. 7, Lauderdale Lakes 33319

(305) 739-9378, Rubin Branch (West Broward county)

Miami:

3000 Biscayne Blvd., Miami 33137

(305) 566-4994

Pompano Beach:

1000 E. Atlantic Blvd., Pompano Beach 33060

(305) 781-5205, Humberto Cruz (North Broward county)

Tallahassee:

110 Florida Press Center, 306 S. Duval St., Tallahassee 32301

(904) 224-6214, Mark Prendergast

Washington, D.C.

Suite 910, 1707 H. St., N.W., Wash., D.C. 20006

(202) 293-9037, William Gibson

HOLLYWOOD SUN-TATTLER

Box 1968, 2600 N. 29th Ave., Hollywood 33022

(305) 929-8100

Fort Lauderdale:

Broward County Courthouse, 201 E. 6 St., Fort Lauderdale 33301

(305) 929-8100

Washington, D.C.:

777 14 St. N.W., Wash., D.C. 20005

(202) 347-7750, B.J. Cutler (Scripps-Howard)

(202) 833-9250, Gayle Tuttle

FLORIDA TIMES-UNION

Box 1949, One Riverside Ave., Jacksonville 32201

(904) 791-4111

The morning Florida Times-Union has a circulation of 160,000 and a Sunday circulation of 210,000.

Larry M. Nichols, state editor, is in charge of the extensive bureau system. Stanton Franklin is Florida editor and Robin Clark is Georgia editor.
Fernandina Beach:

Box 1056, Fernandina Beach 32034

(904) 261-7606, Laura Cianci

(Nassau county)

Gainesville:

Box 214, Gainesville 32601

(904) 373-3581, Nancy Price

(Gainesville and Alachua, Dixie, Gilchrist and Levy counties).

Lake City:

Box 279, Lake City 32055

(904) 752-6111, Ed Stansel

(Lake City, and Columbia, Baker, Suwannee, Lafayette, Union and Hamilton counties)

Madison:

307 South Range St., Madison 32340

(904) 973-2911, Hal Clarendon

(Madison, Jefferson, Taylor and Lafayette)

Palatka:

Box 1304, Palatka 32077

(904) 328-1083, Jack Harper

(Palatka and Putnam counties)

St. Augustine:

40 John St., St. Augustine 32004

(904) 824-2018, Nancy Powell

(St. Augustine, St. Johns and Clay counties)

Starke:

Temple Ave., Starke 32091

(904) 964-8783, Andrea Rowand

(Bradford and Union counties)

Tallahassee:

Box 5623, Tallahassee 32302

(904) 244-7515, Randolph Pendleton, Mike Anderson

(Tallahassee, and Leon, Jefferson, Gadsden, Wakulla, Franklin and Taylor counties)

The extensive bureau system of The Florida Times-Union covers the entire northern and central parts of Florida, and also Southeast Georgia.

Georgia
Brunswick:

>Box 307, Brunswick 31520
>
>(912) 264-0405, Gray Thomas, Walt Stricklin
>
>(Brunswick and Glynn, Camden and McIntosh counties)

Kingsland

>Box 1230, Kingsland 31548
>
>(912) 729-3672, Susan Respes
>
>(Camden County)

Valdosta:

>Box 2505, Valdosta 31601
>
>(912) 242-9900, Jamie Lucke
>
>(Valdosta and Lowndes, Berrien and Colquit counties)

Waycross:

>Box 409, Waycross 30501
>
>(912) 285-8955, Terry Dickson
>
>(Bacon, Charlton, Wayne and Ware counties)

JACKSONVILLE JOURNAL

>One Riverside Ave., Jacksonville 32201
>
>(904) 791-4111

Tallahassee:

>Capital Press, Center Bldg., Tallahassee 32302
>
>(904) 224-7515
>
>This bureau operates only during the legislative session.

NATIONAL ENQUIRER

>Lantana 33464
>
>(305) 586-1111
>
>Circulation of this phenomenal weekly tabloid now is over five million. Editorial operations are centralized.

KNIGHT-RIDDER NEWSPAPERS

>1 Herald Plaza, Miami 33101
>
>(305) 350-2650
>
>Knight-Ridder, formed by a merger of Knight Newspapers and Ridder Publications, consists of 34 daily and 12 other newspapers. Headquarters are in the Miami Herald Building and the Washington bureau is at 1319 F St., N.W., Wash., D.C. 20004.
>
>Local bureaus of the major dailies are listed separately for the Akron Beacon Journal, Charlotte News and Observer, Columbus Ledger and En-quirer, Detroit Free Press, Duluth Herald and News Tribune, Gary Post-Tribune, Grand Forks Herald, Long Beach Independent and Press-Telegram, Miami Herald, Journal of Commerce, Philadelphia Inquirer and News, St. Paul

Dispatch and Pioneer Press, San Jose Mercury-News, Tallahassee Democrat and Wichita Eagle and Beacon.

Other newspapers in this group are the Pasadena (Ca.) Star-News, Boulder (Colo.) Camera, Boca Raton (Fla.) News, Bradenton (Fla.) Herald, Macon (Ga.) Telegraph & News, Fort Wayne (Ind.) News-Sentinel, Lexington (Ky.) Herald and Leader, State College Centre (Pa.) Daily Times and Aberdeen (S.D.) American News.

THE MIAMI HERALD

1 Herald Plaza, Miami 33101

(305) 350-2111

Published in a beautiful modern building on Biscayne Bay, The Miami Herald is one of America's most successful newspapers—in the top five in advertising lineage and the top twenty in circulation. The Herald has the state's largest circulation (407,000 daily and 495,000 Sunday). Several bureaus were opened in recent years as part of the newspaper's coverage of both coasts of southern Florida. Scott Sprein is state editor. In 1980, a bureau was opened in Atlanta. *The Miami News (circ. 61,000, afternoons) is in The Herald building, but has different ownership (Cox).*

Delray Beach:

75 N.E. Federal Hwy., Delray Beach 33444

(305) 272-2626, Lucy Emerson

Ft. Lauderdale:

1520 Sunrise Blvd., Ft. Lauderdale 33304

(305) 462-1550, Carol Weber

Fort Pierce:

114 S. Fourth St., Fort Pierce 33450

(305) 464-3838, Anne Wilder

Key West:

1201 Duval St., Key West 33040

(305) 294-5131, Susan Sachs

Naples:

991 Second Ave. N., Naples 33940

(813) 261-7201, Steve Fishman, David Henry

Stuart:

528 Colorado Ave., Stuart 33494

(305) 287-4030, Chris Spolar, Joe Crankshaw

Tallahassee:

306 Duval St., Tallahassee 32301

(904) 222-3095, Bob Shaw

Vero Beach:

2231 14th Ave., Vero Beach 32960

(305) 562-1746, Phil Long

West Palm Beach:
>   1218 Olive Ave., West Palm Beach 33401
>   (305) 659-6130, Chris Mobley

Atlanta:
>   127 Peachtree St. N.E., Atlanta 30303
>   (404) 525-6677, Willard Rose

Washington, D.C.:
>   1319 F St., N.W., Wash., D.C. 20004
>   (202) 637-3600, Robert Shaw Jr.

TRAVELAGE SOUTHEAST
>   Rm. 303, 7300 Biscayne Blvd., Miami 33138
>   (305) 757-1082, Marilyn Springer
>   See TravelAge in N.Y.C.

MIAMI BUREAUS (area code 305)

Associated Press, I.B.M. Building, 2125 Biscayne Blvd., Miami 33137, 573-7230

Fairchild Publications, 1100 N.E. 125 St., No. Miami 33161

Fort Lauderdale News and Sun-Sentinel, 3000 Biscayne Blvd., Miami 33137, 624-5003

Knight-Ridder Newspapers, 1 Herald Plaza, Miami 33101, 350-2650

Los Angeles Times, 3000 Biscayne Blvd., Miami 33137, Barry Bearak, 757-1531

New York Times, Suite 2806, 100 Biscayne Blvd., Miami 33132, Reginald Stewart, 358-5585

Newsweek, 300 Biscayne Blvd., Miami 33131, Ron Moreau, 358-2541

Orlando Sentinel, Suite 202, 260 N. E. 17 Terrace, Miami 33132, Bob Liff, 372-8957

Reuters, 121 S. E. First St., Miami 33131, Stewart Russell, 374-5013

Travel Weekly, 444 Brickel Ave., Miami 33131, Ernest Blums, 374-1300

Travelage East, 555 N. Birds St., Fort Lauderdale 33304, Marilyn Springer, 945-8778

United Press International, 260 N. E. 17th Terrace, Miami 33132, 373-7685

THE ORLANDO SENTINEL
>   Box 2833, Orlando 32802
>   (305) 420-5411
>   Population of the Orlando Sentinel primary market area is 968,200 for
a 5-county area. Orlando, in Orange county, is close to Disney World and
other tourist attractions. The area's only daily newspaper, the Orlando Sentinel

had a daily circulation in 1983 of 224,000 and a Sunday circulation of 271,000 —an all-time high.

Apopka:
>231 W. Maine St., Apopka 32703
>(305) 886-5161, Ilene Reid
>(West Orange county)

Casselberry:
>100 S. Hwy. 17-92, Casselberry 32707
>(305) 831-1313, Jim Jennings
>(Seminole county)

Clermont:
>300 E. Hwy. 50, Clermont 32711
>(904) 394-3212, Jerry Jackson
>(Lake county)

Cocoa;
>10 Magnolia Ave., Cocoa 32922
>(305) 631-1300, James Fisher
>(Brevard county)

Daytona Beach:
>125 Broadway, Daytona Beach 32016
>(904) 253-1077, Mike McKee
>(Volusia county)

Kissimmee:
>800 Emmett St., Kissimmee 32720
>(904) 734-1404, Kay Vandervoort
>(Volusia county)

Melbourne:
>1918 S. Waverly Place, Melbourne 32935
>(305) 727-2983, Peggy McLaughlin
>(Brevard county)

Miami:
>Suite 202, 260 N.E. 17 Terrace, Miami 33132
>(305) 372-8957, Bob Liff
>(Dade county)

New Smyrna Beach:
>421 Canal St., New Smyrna Beach 32068
>(904) 428-9064, Pat Lamee
>(Volusia county)

Ocoee:
>Suite 1, 304 N. Hwy. 437, Ocoee 32761
>(305) 656-0548, Cindy Spence
>(West Orange county)

Sanford:
>200A N. Park Ave., Sanford 32771
>(305) 322-3513, Jim Robison
>(Seminole county)

Tallahassee:
>306 S. Duval St., Tallahassee 32301
>(904) 222-5564, Larry Lipman
>(Leon county)

Tavares:
>720 Burlingh Blvd., Tavares 32778
>(904) 343-9200, Bill Bond
>(Lake county)

Titusville:
>524 S. Hopkins, Titusville 32780
>(305) 267-2636, Alex Beasley
>(Brevard county)

Winter Park:
>114 E. Comstock, Winter Park 32789
>(305) 647-5110, Gerri Throne
>(North Orange county)

Washington, D.C.
>Suite 910, 1707H St. N.W., Wash., D.C. 20006
>(202) 293-6885, Anne Groer

PALM BEACH POST

>2751 Dixie Hwy., W. Palm Beach 33405
>(305) 833-7411

The morning Post, which has a daily circulation of 95,000 and Sunday circulation of 149,000 (when it's combined with the Evening Times as the Post-Times), closed its bureaus in Belle Glade and Boca Raton and opened a bureau in Okeechobee (on famous Lake Okeechobee).
(Southern Florida area code is 305)

Delray:
>313 N.E. Second Ave., Delray Beach 33444
>272-2646, John Peterson

Ft. Pierce:
>2303 N. Rt. 1, Ft. Pierce 33450
>461-1774, Mary Jo Tierney

Lake Park:
>850 Park Ave., Lake Park 33404
>844-9707, Jamie Prillaman

Lantana:
>505 Lantana Rd., Lantana 33462
>582-6603, Nancy Powell

Okeechobee:

    212 S. Parrott Ave., Okeechobee 33472

    (813) 763-1173, Andrew Garber

Stuart:

    2211 S. Kanner Hwy., Stuart 33459

    287-3947, Sally Swartz

Washington, D.C.:

    1901 Pennsylvania Ave., N.W., Wash., D.C. 20006

    (202) 331-0900, Andy Glass (Cox Newspapers)

ST. PETERSBURG TIMES

    Box 1121, St. Petersburg 33731

    (813) 893-8111

    One of America's finest newspapers, the St. Petersburg Times publishes five local editions for Florida's Gulf coast, with an extensive bureau system.

Bradenton:

    920 Manatee Ave. West, Bradenton 33505

    (813) 746-8086, Elizabeth Kohlman

    (Manatee county)

Brooksville:

    Suite 2-B, 2 Magnolia St., Brooksville 33512

    (904) 796-5751, Bill Stevens

Clearwater:

    710 Court St., Clearwater 33516

    (813) 461-7575, Bob Henderson

    (Clearwater and Upper Pinellas county)

Crystal River:

    Suite 20, Suncoast Plaza, U.S. Highway 19 South, Crystal River 32629

    (904) 795-5252, Teresa Mears

Dade City:

    503 S. 7 St., Dade City 33525

    (904) 567-6836, Jan Gildewell

Inverness:

    205 Courthouse Sq. Inverness 32650

    (904) 344-1266, Teresa Mears

North Suncoast:

    11321 U.S. Highway 19 No., New Port Richey 33568

    (813) 842-9465, John Costa

Tallahassee:

    Florida Press Center, 306 S. Duval St., Tallahassee 32301

    (904) 224-7263, Neil Skene

Tampa:
>Suite 608, 220 Madison St., Tampa 33602
>(813) 223-3435, Frank DeLoache
>(Hillsborough county)

Beaches:
>10681 Gulf Blvd., Treasure Island 33706
>(813) 893-8111, Ed Marks

Washington, D.C.:
>1414-22nd St., N.W., Wash., D.C. 20037
>(202) 296-8583, Charles Stafford

HOSPITAL TOPICS
>Box 5976, Sarasota 34277
>(813) 371-0188

Formerly a monthly in Chicago, this major, 61-year-old publication now enjoys the good life in western Florida as a bimonthly. Consultants and correspondents are in several cities, but editor Gordon Marshall prefers to receive all materials.

TALLAHASSEE DEMOCRAT
>277 N. Magnolia Dr., Tallahassee 32302
>(904) 599-2100

Tallahassee
>306 S. Duval, Tallahassee 32301
>(904) 222-6729, Neil Chetnik

Washington, D.C.:
>1319 F St., N.W., Wash., D.C. 20004
>(202) 637-3600, Jon Peterson (Knight-Ridder Newspapers)

THE TAMPA TRIBUNE
>Box 191, Tampa 33601
>(813) 272-7800

The morning Tribune increased its circulation in 1983 to 191,000. The Tampa Times, an afternoon newspaper, ended publication in 1983. On Sundays, The Tampa Tribune blankets the area with a circulation of 238,000. The newspaper is owned by Media General. Bureaus recently were opened in Bartow and Lakeland.

Bartow:
>130 S. Florida Ave., Bartow 33830
>(813) 533-3157, Marcia Ford

Brandon:
>505 W. Robertson, Brandon 33511
>(813) 685-4581, Mark Gale

Lakeland:
>114 W. Main St., Lakeland 33820
>
>(813) 683-6531, Geoff Nordhoff

Plant City:
>101 N. Wheeler St., Plant City 33566
>
>(813) 754-3763, Donna Smith

Washington D.C.:
>214 Natl. Press Bldg., Wash., D.C. 20045
>
>(204) 347-7770, John Hall

GEORGIA

ATLANTA CONSTITUTION
ATLANTA JOURNAL

>72 Marietta St., N.W., Atlanta 30303
>
>(404) 572-5151

Washington, D.C.:
>1901 Pennsylvania Ave., N.W., Wash., D.C. 20006
>
>(202) 331-0900
>
>Cox Newspaper bureau. Andrew Glass is chief and Bob Dart represents The Atlanta Journal and The Atlanta Constitution.

Though The Atlanta Constitution and Atlanta Journal cover the state of Georgia very thoroughly, these newspapers do not maintain bureaus.

The morning Constitution had a 1983 Monday-to-Friday circulation of 221,000, as compared to the evening Journal's 181,000. The combined Saturday newspaper has a circulation of 432,000 (extraordinary, as Saturday circulation generally is lower than daily) and the Sunday Journal and Constitution has a circulation of 550,000, which is higher than in previous years and one of the 20 largest in the country.

Cox Newspapers is headquartered in Atlanta.

ATLANTA BUREAUS (area code 404)

Apparel News Group, Atlanta Apparel Mart, 250 Spring St., N.W., Atlanta 30303, Leslie Bayler, 688-6830

Associated Press, 500 S. Omni International, Atlanta 30335, Carl Bell, 522-8971

Business Week, 4170 Ashford Dunwoody Rd., Atlanta 30319, Tony Hefferman, 252-0626

Chemical Week, 610 Gas Light Tower, 235 Peachtree St., N.E. Atlanta 30309, Inge Kummant, 521-3287

Chicago Tribune, 907 Cain Tower, Peachtree Center, 229 Peachtree St., Atlanta 30303, Michael Hirsley, 588-1206

Christian Science Monitor, 413 Sinclair Ave., N.E., Atlanta 30307, Robert
 Press, 525-6021
Fairchild Publications, 57 Executive Park South, Suite 380, Atlanta 30329,
 633-9253
Journal of Commerce, 127 Peachtree St., N.E., Suite 827, Atlanta 30303,
 Craig Dunlap, 525-5525
McGraw-Hill World News Service, Suite 610, 235 Peachtree Street, N.E.,
 Atlanta 30319, Inge Kummant, 521-3287
Miami Herald, 127 Peachtree St., N.E., Atlanta 30303, William Rose, 525-6677
Multichannel News, 57 Executive Park South, N.E., Atlanta 30329, Ann
 Dukes, 633-8461
New York Times, 229 Peachtree St., N.E., Atlanta 30303, William Schmidt,
 524-2410
Newsweek, 1120 Gaslight Tower, 235 Peachtree, N.E., Atlanta 30303, Vern
 Smith, 581-0000
Time, Suite 2501, 233 Peachtree St., N.E., Atlanta 30303, Joseph Boyce
 659-8050 Travelage, 40 Peachtree Valley Rd., N.E. Atlanta 30309,
 Nancy Lesure, 351-8362
U.S. News & World Report, 2308 Peachtree Center, S. Tower, 225 Peach-
 tree St., S.E., Atlanta 30303, Linda Lanier, 688-1331
USA Today, Box 77053, Atlanta 30357, John Hesh, 892-1611

United Press International, 1819 Peachtree Rd., N.E., Atlanta 30367,
 355-3700
Wall Street Journal, 6 Piedmont Center, N.E., Atlanta 30305, Eric
 Morgenthaler, 233-2831
Washington Post, Suite 1210, 229 Peachtree St., Atlanta 30303,
 586-9650

THE COLUMBUS ENQUIRER
THE COLUMBUS LEDGER
 Box 711, 17 W. 12 St., Columbus 31902
 (404) 322-8831
 The Enquirer (morning) and Ledger (evening), which previously
operated several bureaus in the state, no longer have bureaus.

HAWAII

HONOLULU ADVERTISER
 Box 3110, Honolulu 96802
 (808) 525-8000
Hawaii county:
 Box 1956, Hilo 96720
 (808) 935-3916, Hugh Clark
Kanai county:
 Box 524, Lihue 96766
 (808) 245-3074, Jan TenBruggencate

Maui county:

> Box 156, Wailuku, Maui 96793
> (808) 244-4880, Ed Tanji

HONOLULU STAR-BULLETIN

> Box 3080, Honolulu 96802
> (802) 525-8607

The evening Star-Bulletin has a larger circulation (112,000) than all of the six other dailies in the state, including its only competitor, The Honolulu Advertiser (83,000), which has the same ownership (Gannett). Both have bureaus on three of the outer islands. On Sundays they combine as the Sunday Star-Bulletin & Advertiser (circulation 195,000).

Hilo:

> Box 81, Hilo 96720
> (808) 935-1012, L.S. Thompson

Kauai:

> 3367 Kuhio Hwy., Lihue 96766
> (808) 245-4146, Lester Chang

Maui:

> 2180 Main St., #618, Wailuku 96793
> (808) 244-3207, Ellen Dyer

Washington, D.C.:

> Box 7858, Wash., D.C. 20044
> (703) 276-5811, Dave Shapiro

IDAHO

IDAHO STATESMAN

> Box 40, 1200 N. Curtis Rd., Boise 83707
> (208) 377-6200

The Idaho Statesman has the state's largest circulation, 57,000 daily and 72,000 Sunday.

Canyon county:

> 1404-A N. Midland Blvd., Nampa 83651
> (208) 466-8918, Miriam Barr

Washington, D.C.:

> 1000 Wilson Blvd., Arlington VA 22209
> (703) 276-5800, Jim Geehan

THE POST-REGISTER

> Box 1800, 333 Northgate Mile, Idaho Falls 83401
> (208) 522-1800
> No bureaus.

ILLINOIS

CHICAGO AND SUBURBS

ADVERTISING AGE
740 N. Rush St., Chicago 60611
(312) 649-5200

Dallas:
5327 N. Central Expy., Dallas 75205
(214) 521-6650, Tom Bayer

Detroit:
965 E. Jefferson Ave., Detroit 48207
(313) 567-9520, Ralph Gray

Los Angeles:
6404 Wilshire Blvd., Los Angeles 90048
(213) 651-3710, Morrie Gelman

New York:
220 E. 42 St., N.Y. 10017
(212) 210-0100, John J. O'Connor

San Francisco area:
4119 Park Blvd., Palo Alto 94306
(415) 858-1247, Stephen Beitler

Washington, D.C.:
Ntl. Press Bldg., Wash., D.C. 20045
(202) 662-7200, Richard L. Gordon

Crain Communications also publishes Automotive News (headquartered in Detroit), Business Insurance (N.Y.), Business Marketing (N.Y.), Modern Healthcare (Chicago), Pensions and Investments (N.Y.), Rubber & Plastics News (Akron), Crain's Chicago Business (Chicago) and Crain's Cleveland Business (Cleveland).

Circulation of Ad Age now is at an all-time high of over 79,000.

AMERICAN MEDICAL NEWS
535 N. Dearborn St., Chicago 60610
(312) 751-6633,

Washington, D.C.:
1101 Vermont Av., N.W., Wash., D.C. 20005
(202) 789-7400, Sharon McIlrath

This publication is an extremely important weekly newspaper, with a circulation of 315,000. It is separate from its affiliated publication, The Journal of the American Medical Association.

BUSINESS INSURANCE
740 N. Rush St., Chicago 60611
(312) 649-5398

Los Angeles:

     6404 Wilshire Blvd., L.A. 90048

     (213) 651-3710, Rhonda L. Rundle

New York:

     220 E. 42 St., New York 10017

     (212) 210-0139, Bill Densmore

Washington, D.C.:

     1253 Ntl. Press Bldg., Wash., D.C. 20045

     (202) 638-5300, Jerry Geisel

     Owned by Crain Communications, this weekly is for corporate and institutional financial executives who purchase insurance and benefit plans.

BUSINESS MARKETING

     740 N. Rush St., Chicago 60611

     (312) 649-5263

     Published by Crain Communications, which also publishes Advertising Age. Formerly called Industrial Marketing.

Detroit:

     965 E. Jefferson Ave., Detroit 48207

     (313) 567-9520, Joseph Bohn

New York:

     220 E. 42nd St., New York 10017

     (212) 210-0100, Bob Donath

Washington, D.C.:

     1253 Ntl. Press Bldg., Wash., D.C. 20045

     (202) 638-5300, Rick Gordon

CHICAGO SUN-TIMES

     401 N. Wabash Ave., Chicago 60611

     (312) 321-3000

Springfield:

     Press Rm., State House Bldg., Springfield 62706

     (217) 753-2986, Michael Briggs

Washington, D.C.:

     708 Ntl. Press Bldg., Wash., D.C. 20045

     (202) 785-8200, Patrick Oster

     With the demise of the afternoon Chicago Daily News on March 4, 1978, the morning Chicago Sun-Times became an all-day newspaper. Daily circulation in 1983 was 639,000, making the newspaper eighth largest in the country, and Sunday circulation was 669,000 (eleventh largest).

     Columnists syndicated by the newspaper include Roger Ebert and Irv Kupcinet for Independent Press Service, Ann Landers, Sydney Harris, Carl Rowan and Rowland Evans/Robert Novak for Field Newspaper Syndicate. In 1983, Rupert Murdoch purchased the newspaper from the Field Brothers.

CHICAGO TRIBUNE

Tribune Tower, 435 N. Michigan Ave., Chicago 60611

(312) 222-3232

The Tribune has maintained its circulation leadership and three of the major reasons are its coverage of the Midwest as a region, longtime reliance on its own national bureaus and extensive suburban coverage. Daily circulation in 1983 was 751,000, and Sunday circulation was 1,116,000, so that The Tribune maintained its position as America's fifth largest newspaper. The leaders are the New York News, Los Angeles Times, New York Post and New York Times.

Nine separate editions are distributed on Monday, Wednesday and Friday to north and south Du Page country, Lake County, Evanston and the North Shore area and five sections of Cook county. The Du Page county editions also are published on Thursday. The combined circulation of suburban Trib is about 362,000.

In 1983, the Trib opened a bureau in Dallas to enhance its status as a national newspaper. Its only bureau in Illinois is in the state capitol.
Springfield:

State House Press Rm., Springfield, IL 62706

(217) 782-6296, Daniel Egler

Atlanta:

907 Cain Tower, Peachtree Center, 229 Peachtree St., Atlanta 30303

(404) 588-1206, Michael Hirsley

Dallas:

8350 N. Central Expy., Dallas 75206

(214) 373-0811, Jim Coates

Denver:

11141 Vrain St., Westminster, CO 80030

(303) 322-3290, James Coates

Los Angeles:

Suite 630, 417 S. Hill St., L.A. 90013

(213) 624-5420, Rogers Worthington

New York:

Suite 2708, 220 E. 42 St., N.Y. 10017

(212) 986-0970, Michael Coakley, Ken Clark

Washington, D.C.:

1707 H St., N.W., Wash., D.C. 20006

(202) 785-9430, Raymond Coffey

Following are the addresses of several Tribune Company columnists:

Jeane Dixon, 1144 18 St., N.W., Wash., D.C. 20036

Charles Goren, 5767 Alton Rd., Miami Beach, FL 33140

Billy Graham, Montreat, NC 28758

Louis Harris, 630 Fifth Ave., N.Y. 10020

Rex Reed, 1 W. 72 St., N.Y. 10023

THE DAILY CALUMET

9120 S. Baltimore, Chicago 60617

(312) 375-2000

No bureaus.

DECATUR HERALD and REVIEW

Box 311, 601 E. William St., Decatur 62525

(217) 429-5151

The evening edition was terminated in 1982. The morning circulation is 54,000 (57,000 on Sunday). Decatur is in central Illinois.

Clinton:

505 Westside Sq., Clinton 61727

(217) 935-8877, Norm Lewis

Mattoon:

1519 Broadway, Mattoon 61938

(217) 234-2210, Mark Kinders

Springfield:

Press room, Statehouse, Springfield 62706

(217) 787-4043, Mike Lawrence (Lee Newspapers)

HARDWARE MERCHANDISER

7300 N. Cicero Ave., Lincolnwood 60646

(312) 588-7300

Largest circulation in the hardware field. Contents page lists names and addresses of regional managers, which are sales offices. No bureaus. Published by The Irving-Cloud Publishing Company.

Other Irving-Cloud publications are Dental Products Report, Hardlines Wholesaling, Heavy Duty Equipment Maintenance, Jobber Topics, Super Service Station, Warehouse Distribution, Fleet Maintenance and Dental Lab Products.

INDUSTRIAL RESEARCH/DEVELOPMENT

1301 S. Grove Ave., Barrington 60010

(312) 381-1840

No bureaus, though editor Robert Jones has many correspondents. Circulation 101,000. Technical Publishing Co. (owned by The Dun & Bradstreet Corporation) also publishes The American Journal of Medicine, Consulting Engineer, Control Engineering, Datamation, Dun's Review, Electric Light & Power, Fire Engineering, Graphic Arts Monthly, Highway & Heavy Construction, Mining Equipment International, Plant Engineering, Pollution Engineering, Power Engineering, Purchasing World, Water & Wastes Engineering.

All are located at company headquarters in Barrington (suburban Chicago) except Datamation (Greenwich, Conn.) and The American Journal of Medicine, Dun's Review, Fire Engineering, Graphics Arts Monthly, Mining Equipment International, Water & Wastes Engineering and World Construction (N.Y.)—all of which are at 666 Fifth Ave., N.Y. 10103.

LEADER NEWSPAPERS
POST NEWSPAPERS

3148 N. Central Ave., Chicago 60634

(312) 889-5200

Founded by Hubert F. Messé (Messé Newspapers, Inc.). These two chains publish 17 weekly newspapers in and near Chicago, The Leader Newspapers are the: Belmont Central Leader, West Belmont Leader, Portage Park Leader, Jefferson Park Leader, Mayfair Leader, Bel-Park Leader, Cragin Leader, Harlem Irving Leader, Northwest Leader and Suburban Leader.

The Post Newspapers are: The Northlake Post, Elmwood Park Post, River Grove Post, Franklin Park Post, Schiller Park Post and Mont Clare Post.

JET

820 S. Michigan Ave., Chicago 60605

(312) 322-9200

Los Angeles:

3600 Wilshire Blvd., L.A. 90010

(213) 386-5200, Aldore Collier

New York:

1270 Ave. of the Americas, N.Y. 10020

(212) 586-2911

Washington, D.C.:

1750 Pennsylvania Ave., N.W., Wash., D.C. 20006

(202) 393-5860, Simeon Booker

Johnson Publishing Co. also publishes Ebony, which utilizes the same bureaus as Jet, the weekly news magazine.

MODERN SALON

Box 400, Prairie View 60069

(312) 634-2600

Editor Lorry Delany reports that the news section is different in each of the five editions (East, Midwest, South, West and Canada) and local news should be sent to the news editor at the main office.

OFFICE PRODUCTS DEALER

Hithcock Bldg., Wheaton 60188

(312) 665-1000

No bureaus. Hitchcock Publishing Company (a subsidiary of American Broadcasting Companies) also publishes Assembly Engineering, Industrial Finishing, Infosystems, Machine and Tool Bluebook and Quality.

PLAYBOY

919 N. Michigan Ave., Chicago 60611

(312) 751-8000

Playboy has the largest circulation of any men's magazine—over 4,500,000.

Los Angeles:

8560 Sunset Blvd., L.A. 90048

(213) 659-4080

New York:

747 Third Avenue, N.Y. 10017

(212) 688-3030, G. Barry Golson (N.Y. office includes the fashion editor).

RESTAURANTS & INSTITUTIONS

1350 E. Touhy Ave., Des Plaines 60018

(312) 653-8800

Controlled (free) circulation of this major semi-monthly magazine has increased to over 107,000.

West Coast:

411 Tenth St., Santa Monica CA 90402

(213) 451-2660, Barbara Dawson

Washington:

Suite 639, 1435 G St., N.W., Wash., D.C. 20005

(202) 628-2773, Sylvia Riggs

TRAVELAGE MIDAMERICA

2416 Prudential Plaza, Chicago 60601

(312) 861-0432

See TravelAge East, N.Y.C.

CHICAGO BUREAUS (area code 312)

American Banker, 53 W. Jackson Blvd., Chicago 60604, 427-4347

Amusement Business, 150 N. Wacker Dr., Chicago 60606, Jim Helmer, 236-9818

Apparel News Group, The Apparel Center, 350 N. Orleans, Chicago 60654, Paula Lashinsky, 670-2230

Associated Press, 230 N. Michigan Ave., Chicago 60601, Thomas Dyyard, 781-0500

Automotive Industries, 100 S. Wacker Dr., Chicago 60606, John Furwalter, 782-1400

Automotive News, 740 N. Rush St., Chicago 60611, Susan Gurewity, 676-4473

Back Stage, 841 N. Addison Ave., Elmhurst 60126, Will Anderson, 834-7533

Business Week, 645 N. Michigan Ave., Chicago 60611, Mark Morrison, 751-3813

Cash Box, 29 E. Madison St., Chicago 60602, Camille Compasio, 346-7272

Chemical & Engineering News, 176 W. Adams St., Chicago 60603, Ward Worthy, 236-7325

Chemical Week, 645 N. Michigan Ave., Chicago 60611, Jeff Ryser, 751-3700

Christian Science Monitor, 203 N. Wabash Ave., Chicago 60602, Lucia Movat, 726-7640

Dun's Business Month, 303 E. Wacker Dr., Chicago 60601, Lynn Atkins, 938-2935

Editor & Publisher, 303 E. Ohio St., Chicago 60611, 565-0123

Electronics, 645 N. Michigan Ave., Chicago 60611, Wesley Iverson, 751-3824

Fairchild Publications, 11 E. Adams St., Chicago 60603, Ann Keeton, Maria Paul, 663-3500

Food Engineering, 100 S. Wacker Dr., Chicago 60606, Charles Morris, 782-1400

Forbes, 1064 Wrigley Bldg., 410 N. Michigan Ave., Chicago 60611, Jill Bettner, 329-1562

Gralle Publications, 3525 W. Peterson Ave., Chicago 60659, 463-1102

Industry Week, 2 Illinois Center Bldg., Chicago 60601, Brian Moskal, 861-0880

Iron Age, 100 S. Wacker Dr., Chicago 60606, Keith Bennett, 782-1400

Journal of Commerce, 77 W. Washington St., Chicago 60602, 786-9426

Los Angeles Times, 435 N. Michigan Ave., Chicago 60611, Larry Green, 467-4670

McGraw-Hill World News Service, 645 N. Michigan Ave., Chicago 60611, Jeff Ryser, 751-3700

Medical World News, 1143 West Pratt, Chicago 60626, Judy Alsengrom, 274-6580

Merchandising, 3525 W. Peterson Ave., Chicago 60659, Debbie Rosenblum, 463-1102

New York Times, 11 East Walton Pl., Chicago 60611, Andrew H. Malcolm, 658-5915

Newsweek, 200 E. Randolph Dr., Chicago 60601, Frank Maier, 861-1180

People, 303 E. Ohio St., Chicago 60611, Linda Witt, 329-6800

Reuters, 141 W. Jackson Blvd., Chicago 60604, Felix Seigio, 922-6030

Time, 303 E. Ohio St., Chicago 60611, Christopher Ogden, 329-7860

Travel Weekly, R.D. 4, Monmouth 61462, Robert Grimsley, 734-5014.

Travelage, 2416 Prudential Plaza, Chicago 60601, Linda Smith Jessup, 861-0432

U.S. News & World Report, 1433 Tribune Sq. 435 N. Michigan Ave., Chicago
60611, Michael Bose, Mary Galligan, 329-0890

USA Today, 6 N. Michigan Ave., Chicago 60602, Steve Wilson,
263-2591

United Press International, 360 N. Michigan Ave., Chicago 60611
781-1600

Variety, 400 N. Michigan Ave., Chicago 60611, Morry Roth, 337-4984

Wall Street Journal, 200 W. Monroe St., Chicago 60603, A. Richard Martin,
648-7600

Washington Post, Rm. 519-A, 401 N. Wabash Ave., Chicago 60611,
321-3000

SPRINGFIELD BUREAUS (area code 217)

All of the bureaus are on the third floor of the State Capitol, Springfield 62706. UPI also is at 500 E. Monroe St. and AP is at Lincoln Tower Bldg.
The State Journal-Register is at 313 S. 6 St.

Associated Press		789-2700
Chicago Sun-Times	Michael Biggs	753-2986
Chicago Tribune	Daniel Egler	782-6296
Copley Newspapers	Ray Serati	544-3666
Gannett	James George	782-6292
Lee Enterprises	Mike Lawrence	789-0865
St. Louis Post-Dispatch	William Lambrecht	525-4912
United Press		525-2326

INDIANA

THE POST-TRIBUNE

1065 Broadway, Gary 46402

(219) 881-3000

Crown Point:

112 W. Clark St., Crown Point 46307

(219) 663-0060

Indianapolis:

Rm. 4H, Statehouse, Indianapolis 46204

(317) 631-7400, Robert Ashley

Merrillville:

23 West 80th Place, Merrillville 46410

(219) 769-0243, Guy Slaughter

Valparaiso:

58 W. Lincolnway, Valparaiso 46383

Washington, D.C.:
> 1319 F St., N.W., Wash., D.C. 20004
> (202) 637-3600, Charlie Green (Knight-Ridder Newspapers)

HARDWARE RETAILING
> 770 N. High St., Indianapolis 46224
> (317) 248-1261
> Published by the National Retail Hardware Association, Hardware
Retailing lists the names and addresses of Regional Managers on its contents
page. However, these are sales representatives and are not news bureaus.

THE INDIANAPOLIS NEWS
> 307 Pennsylvania St., Indianapolis 46204
> (317) 633-1240
Bloomington (Indiana University):
> 661 N. Walnut St., Bloomington 47401
> (812) 336-6841, William L. Pittman
Lafayette (Purdue University)
> 201 Main St., Lafayette 47902
> (317) 742-4029, Norman Bess
Washington, D.C.:
> 641 Natl. Press Bldg., Wash., D.C. 20045
> (202) 638-2425, Louis C. Hiner
> Mr. Hiner also represents the Muncie Press in Indiana and the
Phoenix Gazette and the Indianapolis News.

THE INDIANAPOLIS STAR
> 307 N. Pennsylvania St., Indianapolis 46204
> (317) 633-1240
> Circulation increased in 1983 to 225,000 daily and 370,000 Sunday,
largest in the state. Bureaus in Bloomington and Lafayette were closed.
Washington, D.C.:
> 641 Ntl. Press Bldg., Wash., D.C. 20045
> (202) 638-6425, Benjamin R. Cole
> Mr. Cole also represents the Muncie Star in Indiana and The Arizona
Republic in Phoenix.

THE JOURNAL-GAZETTE
> Box 88, 600 West Main St., Fort Wayne 46801
> (219) 461-8253
> No bureaus.

IOWA

BETTER HOMES & GARDENS
1716 Locust St., Des Moines 50336
(515) 284-9011
Circulation is 8 million! Meredith Corporation also publishes Metropolitan Home and Successful Farming.

New York:
750 Third Ave., N.Y. 10017
(212) 557-6600, Margaret Daly, George Bush

DES MOINES REGISTER
715 Locust St., Des Moines 50304
(515) 284-8000
With a daily circulation of 250,000 and a Sunday circulation of about 400,000, "The Register is Iowa." The evening Tribune merged into The Register on September 27, 1982. Bureaus were closed in Clive and Sioux City and a bureau was opened in Ames.

Ames:
415½ Clark Ave., Ames 50010
(515) 232-3560, Willis David Hoover

Cedar Rapids:
414 Guaranty Bldg., 216 Third St., S.E., Cedar Rapids
(319) 365-7474, John Carlson, Harry Baumert

Davenport:
424 Union Arcade Bldg., Davenport 52801
(319) 326-2662, William Ryberg

Dubuque:
667 Fischer Bldg., Dubuque 52001
(319) 583-5655, Kenneth Pins

Iowa City:
500 Iowa State Bank Bldg. 102 Clinton St., Iowa City
(319) 351-6257, Tom Knudson

Waterloo:
Sycamore 501 Bldg. Room 641, Waterloo 50703
(319) 233-2018, Jack Hovelson

Washington, D.C.:
1317 F St., N.W. Wash., D.C. 20004
(202) 347-9111, James Risser

KANSAS

TOPEKA CAPITAL-JOURNAL
616 Jefferson, Topeka 66607

(913) 295-1111

Lawrence:

3203 W. 21 Pl., Lawrence 66044

(913) 842-4290, Sherry Pigg

Manhattan:

530 Kearney, Manhattan 66502

(913) 539-1447, Rita Shelley

Missouri

Kansas City:

1305 S. 21 St., Blue Springs, MO 64015

(816) 229-9580, Alan Eskew

Washington, D.C.:

605 14 St., N.W., Wash., D.C. 20004

(202) 783-3274, Ken Peterson

WICHITA EAGLE-BEACON
825 E. Douglas, Wichita 67202

(316) 268-6000

The morning Eagle-Beacon (circulation 122,000) is the state's largest circulation newspaper. In 1980, Knight-Ridder merged the afternoon Beacon into the Eagle. Sunday circulation in 1983 was an all-time high, 185,000.

Topeka:

Press Room, State Capital, Topeka 66601

(913) 296-3006, Terry Wooten

Washington, D.C.:

1319 F St., N.W., Wash., D.C. 20004

(202) 637-3600, Robert S. Boyd

KENTUCKY

THE COURIER-JOURNAL
525 West Broadway, Louisville 40202

(502) 582-4011

The morning Courier-Journal has the state's largest circulation (179,000). The evening Times (139,000) is published by the same company. Bary Bingham Jr. is the famous editor and publisher of both. The Sunday Courier-Journal and Times has a circulation of 321,000.

The Courier-Journal has an extensive bureau system in Kentucky and nearby Indiana.

Indiana

Bardstown:
> Box 460, Bardstown 40004
> (502) 348-4247, Al Cross

Frankfort:
> 614B Shelby St., Frankfort 40601
> (502) 875-5136, Rich Whitt

Hazard (East Kentucky):
> Box 1132, Hazard 41701
> (606) 476-8611, Ralph Dunlop

Lexington:
> 314 Old East Vine, Lexington 40507
> (606) 254-7888, Bob Garrett

Somerset:
> Box 74, Somerset 42501
> (606) 679-8735, Carol Cropper

W. Kentucky:
> 603 Oaklawn Dr., Paducah 42001
> (502) 554-3448, Bill Powell

Kentucky

Indianapolis:
> ISTA Bldg., Indianapolis 46204
> (317) 634-1872, Gordon Engelhart

New Albany:
> 419 W. First St., New Albany 47150
> (812) 948-1315, Linda Stahl

Washington, D.C.:
> 968 Ntl. Press Bldg., Wash., D.C. 20045
> (202) 628-7704, Mike Brown

LOUISVILLE TIMES
> 525 W. Broadway, Louisville 40202
> (502) 582-4641

Frankfort:
> 614-B Shelby St., Frankfort 40601
> (502) 875-1111, Lonnie Rosenwald

New Albany:
> 419 W. First St., New Albany, IN 47150
> (812) 945-5271, Clay Ryce

LOUISIANA

THE TIMES-PICAYUNE/THE STATES-ITEM
3800 Howard Ave., New Orleans 70140

(504) 586-3560

The morning Times-Picayune and afternoon States-Item combined into an all-day newspaper. In 1983, The Times-Picayune/The States-Item had a five-day daily circulation of 278,365; Saturday, 250,000, and Sunday, 332,000, all of which are the largest circulation in the state.

Baton Rouge:

Box 44122, Baton Rouge 70804

(504) 383-4619, Jack Wardlaw

Jefferson Parish (East Bank):

3841 Veterans Memorial Blvd., Metairie 70002

(504) 586-3674, James Gill

River Parishes:

Suite E, 100 Ormond Blvd., La Place 70068

(504) 652-6849, Mary Heffron

St. Bernard Parish:

9212 West Judge Perez Dr., Chalmette 70043

(504) 586-3533, Gene Mearns

St. Tammany Parish:

Suite 102, 1508 Gause Blvd., Slidell 70458

(504) 366-5353, Bruce Nolan

West Bank:

16 West Bank Expressway, Gretna 70053

(504) 366-5353, Bruce Nolan

Washington, D.C.:

1029 Natl. Press Bldg., Wash., D.C. 20045

(202) 383-7824, Edgar Poe (Newhouse News Service)

THE SHREVEPORT TIMES
222 Lake St., Shreveport 71130

(318) 459-3200

Baton Rouge:

State Capitol, Baton Rouge 70804

(504) 342-7333, John Hill

Natchitoches:

111 E. 5 St., Natchitoches 71457

(318) 352-9605, Kathy Downs

Ruston:

101 S. Trenton St., Ruston 71270

(318) 255-3902, Gary Walker

Washington, D.C.:

Box 7858, Wash., D.C. 20044

(703) 276-5800, Mike Meacham

MAINE

BANGOR DAILY NEWS

Box 1329, 491 Main St., Bangor 04401

(207) 942-4881

(Maine area code is 207)

Augusta:

Room 400, Station 50, State House, Augusta 04333

289-3158, Davis Rawson

Ellsworth:

Box 727, 96 Main St., Ellsworth 04605

667-9393, Jean Hay

Houlton:

6 Randall Av., Houlton 04730

532-9257, Mrs. Virginia Hiltz

Machias:

Box 145, 85 Main St., Machias 04654

255-3324

Madawaska:

Box 192, 6 Tenth Av., Madawaska 04756

728-6501, Beurmond Banville

Presque Isle:

Box 248, 495 Main St., Presque Isle 04769

768-5681, Dean Rhodes

Rockland:

Box 276, 419 Main St., Rockland 04841

596-6688, Theodore Sylvester Jr.

Skowhegan:

Box 8, 150 Water St., Showhegan 04976

474-3355, Bruce Hertz

Washington, D.C.:

1220 Maryland Ave., N.E., Wash., D.C. 20002

(202) 398-5637, John S. Day

This extensive bureau system is under the direction of David Bright, Maine editor, The morning News is the largest daily newspaper (80,000) in Northern New England and has a weekend circulation of 92,000. This indeed is extraordinary since the population of Bangor is 32,000, about half that of Portland (62,000). The bureau system enables the News to cover a large area. Another reason is that there are no other dailies in the eight counties which the newspaper serves.

EVENING EXPRESS
PORTLAND PRESS HERALD

390 Congress St., Portland 04101

(207) 775-5811

(Maine area code is 207)

Biddeford-Saco:

5 Washington St., Biddeford 04005

283-3605, Sid Leavitt

Brunswick-Bath:

114 Maine St., Brunswick 04011

725-8795, Paul Downing

Rockland:

445 Main St., Rockland 04841

594-5571, Larry Ouellette

Sanford:

221 Main St., Sanford 04073

324-5222, C. Scott Hoar

Portland is the headquarters of the Guy Gannett Publishing Co. Mrs. Jean Gannett Hawley is president of this group, which includes the Waterville Morning Sentinel and Kennebec Journal in Augusta. These Maine newspapers are not part of the Gannett chain, which is headquartered in Rochester, N.Y.

The Maine Sunday Telegram (circulation of over 125,000) is separately staffed in the same building.

MARYLAND

THE CAPITAL

213 West St., Annapolis 21404

(301) 268-5000

No bureaus.

BALTIMORE NEWS-AMERICAN

301 E. Lombard St., Baltimore 21202

(301) 752-1212

The afternoon News-American recently reopened bureaus in Annapolis (the Arundel county bureau), Towson (Baltimore county), Bel Air (Harford county), and Ellicott City (Howard county). The News-American daily circulation in 1983 was 138,000, and the Sunday circulation was 185,000, both smaller than in previous years.

Annapolis:

Press Room, State House, Annapolis 21404

(301) 269-0761

Washington, D.C.:

1701 Pennsylvania Ave., N.W., Wash., D.C. 20006

(202) 298-6920, Joseph Kingsbury Smith

(Hearst Newspapers)

BALTIMORE SUN

Calvert & Centre Sts., Baltimore 21203

(301) 332-6000

World-renowned for its national and international news coverage (and for such famous journalists of the past as H.L. Mencken), the Baltimore Sun is a successful locally owned company which also concentrates on coverage of its local area. Daily circulation is 183,000 (morning Sun) and 167,000 (evening Sun), and Sunday circulation increased to 393,000, larger than any other newspaper in the state. Independent Press Service syndicates features and news from the Sun.

Annapolis:

60 West St., Annapolis 21404

(301) 269-0153

Baltimore county:

401 Washington Ave., Towson 21204

(301) 296-1170

Bel Air:

45 N. Main St., Bel Air 21014

(301) 838-7425

Carroll county:

39 Court Pl., Westminster 21157

(201) 848-2474

Howard county:

3146 Rogers Ave., Ellicott City 21043

(301) 461-9673

Wicomico county (Eastern Shore):

c/o Baltimore Sun, Baltimore 21273

(301) 742-7797

Washington, D.C.:

1627 K St., N.W., Wash., D.C. 20006

(202) 347-8250, Ernest Furguson Jr.

The Sun maintains one of the largest bureaus in Washington serving a single newspaper. Mr. Furguson's column is syndicated by the Los Angeles Times.

MASSACHUSETTS

BOSTON GLOBE

135 Morrissey Blvd., Boston 02107

(617) 929-3000

The state's largest circulation newspaper. The Globe now is published all day, with a circulation of 515,000 which is the 13th largest circulation newspaper in the U.S. The Sunday Globe is the 9th largest, with a circulation of 782,000.

City Hall:

> State House, Boston 02133
> (617) 929-2596

Washington, D.C.:

> 1750 Pennsylvania Ave., N.W., Wash., D.C. 20006
> (202) 393-6020

BOSTON HERALD

> 300 Harrison Ave., Boston 02106
> (617) 426-3000
>
> In 1982, Rupert Murdoch purchased the Boston Herald American

from Hearst and proceeded to make many changes, including switching to a tabloid format with a colorful style almost identical to the New York Post (also owned by Murdoch). The formula has not been as successful as in New York, and the Herald remains far behind the Boston Globe in circulation.

City Hall:

> City Hall, Boston 02201
> (617) 725-4000, (617) 426-3000, ext. 416

Federal Bldg.:

> Post Office Square, Boston 02109
> (617) 223-7121, (617) 426-3000, ext. 419

State Capitol:

> State House, Boston 02133
> (617) 727-2495, (617) 426-3000, ext. 418

Washington, D.C.:

> 533 Natl. Press Bldg., Wash., D.C. 20045
> (202) 313-1531, Niles Lathem

CAHNERS PUBLISHING COMPANY

> 221 Columbus Ave., Boston 02116
> (617) 536-7780
>
> All of the Cahners Publications are represented in Washington, D.C.,
> at 968 Ntl. Press Bldg., Wash., D.C. 20045
> (202) 628-2773, David Heinly
>
> The Cahners Publications are grouped and located as follows:

Boston: 221 Columbus Ave., Boston 02116, (617) 536-7780

> Design News
> EDN
> Electronic Business
> Mini-Micro Systems
> Modern Materials Handling
> Plastics World
> Purchasing
> Traffic Management

Chicago: 1350 E. Touhy Ave., Des Plaines 60018, (312) 635-8800
        Appliance Manufacturer
        Brick & Clay Record
        Building Design & Construction
        Building Supply News
        Ceramic Industry
        Construction Equipment
        Construction Equipment Maintenance
        Foodservice Distribution News
        Foodservice Equipment Specialist
        Restaurants and Institutions
        Package Engineering
        Professional Builder/Apartment Business
        Security World
        Security Distributing & Marketing
        Service World International
        Specifying Engineer
New York: 205 E. 42 St., N.Y. 10017, (212) 949-4400
        Electro Procurement, Recreational Industry and other New York-based
publications of Cahners no longer are published.

THE CHRISTIAN SCIENCE MONITOR
        One Norway St., Boston 02115
        (617) 262-2300
Atlanta:
        413 Sinclair Ave., N.E., Atlanta 30307
        (404) 525-6021, Robert Press
Chicago:
        203 N. Wabash Ave., Chicago 60602
        (312) 726-7640, Lucia Mouat
Los Angeles:
        5225 Wilshire Blvd., L.A. 90036
        (213) 932-1260, Marshall Ingwerson
New York:
        220 E. 42 St., Suite 3006, N.Y. 10017
        (212) 599-1850, John Yemma
Washington, D.C.:
        910 16 St., N.W., Wash., D.C. 20006
        (202) 785-4400, Charlotte Saikowski

        The importance of the Monitor is not indicated by its circulation, a
modest 145,000, which is lower than in past years, but rather by the fact that
it is an internationally prestigious newspaper which is extremely influential.
Distribution of the Monitor to libraries and Christian Science reading rooms

undoubtedly produces a sizeable number of readers per copy, but the major bonus is The Christian Science Monitor News Service, which is distributed by the Los Angeles Times Syndicate to major newspapers.

COMPUTERWORLD
375 Cochituate Rd., Rt. 30, Framingham 01701
(617) 879-0700
Western:
407 California Ave., Palo Alto 94306
(415) 328-8064, Jeffrey Beeler
New York:
401 E. 80 St., N.Y. 10021
(212) 570-2135, David Myers
Washington, D.C.:
821 Ntl. Press Bldg., Wash., D.C. 20045
(202) 347-6718, Jake Kirchner

BOSTON BUREAUS (area code 617)

Associated Press, 184 High St., Boston 02110,
357-8100

Business Week, McGraw-Hill Bldg., Copley Sq., Boston 02116, Emily Smith,
262-1160

Commercial & Financial Chronicle, 4 Water St., Arlington 02174, C. Peter
Jorgensen, 643-7900

Datamation, 1 Chaucer Rd., RFD # 2, Sandwich 02563, Ralph Emmett,
888-6312

Electronics, McGraw-Hill Bldg., 607 Boylston St., Boston 02116, Linda Lowe,
Normal Alster, 262-1160

Fairchild Publications, 480 Boylston St., Boston 02116, 267-8282

New York Times, 15 Court Sq., Boston 02108, Fox Butterfield,
720-0727

Newsweek, 185 Dartmouth St., Boston 02116, Sylvester Monroe,
262-5232

People, 302 Berkley St., Boston 02116, Gail Jennens, 247-4769

Time, 277 Dartmouth St., Boston 02216, 262-7551

United Press International, 20 Ashburton Pl., Boston 02108, 226-4000

United States Banker, Box 2386, Woburn 01888, John Clark, 938-9009

Wall Street Journal, 35 Congress St., Boston 02109, June Kronkolz,
742-5600

THE SPRINGFIELD UNION
THE DAILY NEWS
SUNDAY REPUBLICAN

      1860 Main St., Springfield 01102

      (413) 788-1300

(Western Mass. telephone area code is 413)

Chicopee:

      247 Exchange St., Chicopee 01013

      592-2377; 788-1322, June Greig

Enfield:

      77 Hazard Ave., Enfield 06082

      (203) 745-0309, Charlotte Libov

Palmer:

      448 N. Main St., Palmer 01069

      283-6361, 788-1020, Elsie Osterman

Westfield:

      132 Elm St., Westfield 01075

      562-2951; 788-1321, Cynthia Simison

THE EVENING GAZETTE
WORCESTER TELEGRAM

      20 Franklin St., Worcester 01613

      (617) 793-9100

      (Eastern Mass. telephone area code is 617)

Athol:

      507 Main St., Athol 01331

      249-6163

      (Athol, Orange, Petersham, Phillipston)

Boston:

      Room 456, State House, Boston 02133

      523-2514

Clinton:

      358 High St., Clinton 01510

      365-2462

      (Clinton, Lancaster, Sterling)

Fitchburg:

      580 Main St., Fitchburg 01420

      343-4836

      (Fitchburg, Ashby, Townsend, Lunenburg, Ayer, Pepperell, Groton, Littleton, Shirley)

Gardner:

      90 Main St., Gardner 01440

      632-1800

      (Gardner, Ashburnham, Hubbardston, Templeton, Westminster)

Leominster:

      18 Main St., Leominster 01453

      534-4921

      (Leominster and Harvard)

Marlboro:

      110 Pleasant St., Marlboro 01752

      485-2135

      (Marlboro, Northboro, Hudson, Bolton, Berlin, Framingham, Acton, Boxboro, Stow, Maynard)

Milford:

      2 Central St., Milford 01757

      473-0262

      (Milford, Hopedale, Bellingham, Franklin, Medway and Millis)

Northbridge:

      1035 Providence Rd., Northbridge 01534

      234-5882

      (Northbridge, Sutton, Upton)

Southbridge:

      51 Central St., Southbridge 01550

      764-2519

      (Southbridge, Charlton, Sturbridge, Brimfield, Wales, Holland)

Spencer:

      122 Main St., Spencer 01562

      885-3900

      (Spencer, New Braintree, Oakham, Brookfield, North Brookfield, Warren, East Brookfield, West Brookfield, Ware, Hardwick, Barre)

Uxbridge:

      27 S. Main St., Uxbridge 01569

      278-3522

      (Uxbridge, Douglas, Mendon, Millville, Blackstone)

Webster:

      27 South Main St., Webster 01570

      943-5400

Westboro:

      10 South St., Westboro 01581

      366-5955

      (Westboro, Southboro, Hopkinton)

Winchendon:

      24 Spring St., Winchendon 01475

      297-1015

      (Royalston, Winchendon)

In addition to this extensive bureau system in Massachusetts, the Worcester Telegram and Gazette maintains two other bureaus.

Connecticut:
>5 Bundy St., Putnam 06260
>(203) 928-2252
>(Putnam, Woodstock, Killingly, Thompson)

Washington, D.C.:
>1237 Ntl. Press Bldg., Wash., D.C. 20045
>(202) 554-3579, Betty Mills
>(Griffin-Larrabee, News Bureau)

MICHIGAN

BATTLE CREEK ENQUIRER
>155 W. Van Buren St., Battle Creek 49016
>(616) 964-7161

Lansing:
>106 W. Allegan St., Lansing 48064
>(517) 485-1793, Jerry Moskal

Washington, D.C.:
>1000 Wilson Blvd. Arlington VA 22209
>(703) 276-5800, James Geehan

Federated Publications, which includes the Boise Daily Statesman in Idaho, Lafayette Journal and Courier and Marion Courier Tribune in Indiana; Lansing State Journal in Michigan, and Bellingham Herald and Olympia Daily Olympian in Washington, is part of the Gannett group.

AUTOMOTIVE NEWS
>965 E. Jefferson Ave., Detroit 48207
>(313) 567-9520

Chicago:
>740 N. Rush St., Chicago 60611
>(312) 676-4473, Susan Gurevitz

Los Angeles:
>6404 Wilshire Blvd., L.A. 90048
>(213) 651-3710, Matt DeLorenzo

New York:
>220 E. 42 St., N.Y. 10017
>(212) 210-0100, John Russell

Washington, D.C.:
>515 Ntl. Press Bldg., Wash., D.C. 20045
>(202) 638-5300, Helen Kahn

Resident correspondents in 57 U.S. cities.

DETROIT FREE PRESS

321 W. Lafayette Blvd., Detroit 48231

(313) 222-6600

Suburban Editions

Oakland:

1185 S. Adams Rd., Birmingham 48011

(313) 540-6600, Mike Wagner

Macomb:

55 Church St., Mt. Clemens 48043

(313) 523-2512, Kathy O'Gorman

Other Bureaus

Lansing:

820 Washington Sq. Bldg., Lansing 48933

(417) 372-8860, Tim Jones

Washington, D.C.:

1195 Ntl. Press Bldg., Wash., D.C. 20045

(202) 637-3600, Bob Boyd (Knight-Ridder)

Western:

259 Linden Drive, Boulder, CO 80302

(303) 440-4931, Gary Blonston

THE DETROIT NEWS

615 Lafayette Blvd., Detroit 48231

(313) 222-2000

Formerly an evening newspaper, The Detroit News has followed the trend of other evening newspapers and now publishes all-day in order to compete with the morning Free Press. Daily circulation increased in 1983 to 651,000. Thus, the News is one of the nation's biggest circulation newspapers and ahead of the Free Press (635,000). On Sundays, the News has increased its circulation to 859,000, which is seventh biggest in the country and well ahead of the Free Press (788,000).

Following is the extensive bureau system:

Oakland County:

925 East Maple, Birmingham 48011

(313) 645-0340, Doug Ilka

City-County:

1108 City-County Bldg., Detroit 48226

(313) 222-2396, Ric Bohy

Ann Arbor:

202 E. Washington St., Ann Arbor 48104

(313) 222-2750, Oli Hanninen

Garden City:

2440 Middle Belt, Garden City 48135

(313) 522-2500, Howard Warren

Lansing:
>> 101 S. Washington, Lansing 48933
>> (517) 371-3660, Joanna Firestone

Mt. Clemens:
>> 56 Macomb Pl., Mt. Clemens 48043
>> (313) 468-0528, Joan Walter

Pontiac:
>> 1200 North Telegraph, Pontiac 48056
>> (313) 338-0319, Bob Roach

Washington, D.C.:
>> 425 Ntl. Press Bldg., Wash., D.C. 20045
>> (202) 628-4566, Gary Schuster

DETROIT BUREAUS (area code 313)

Advertising Age, 965 E. Jefferson Ave., Detroit 48207, Ralph Gray,
>> 567-9520

Associated Press, 660 Plaza Dr., Detroit 48226, 965-9500

Automotive Industries, 2600 Fisher Bldg., Detroit 48202, Joseph Callahan,
>> John McElroy, 875-2090

Business Marketing, 965 E. Jefferson Ave., Detroit 48207, Joseph Bohn,
>> 567-9520

Business Week, 3756 City Natl. Bank Bldg., Detroit 48226, William Hampton,
>> 962-5600

Chemical Week, 3756 City Natl. Bank Bldg., Detroit 48226, David Whiteside,
>> James Schwartz, 962-5600

Commercial Car Journal, 2600 Fisher Bldg., Detroit 48202, Joseph Cobb,
>> 875-2090

Fairchild Publications, New Center Bldg., Detroit 48202, 871-7150

Iron Age, 2600 Fisher Bldg., Detroit 48202, B. H. Berry, 875-2090

Los Angeles Times, 615 Griswold St., Detroit 48226, Donald Woutak,
>> 965-4570

McGraw-Hill World News Service, 3756 City Natl. Bank Bldg., Detroit 48226,
>> David Whiteside, 962-5600

Motor Magazine, 29226 Orchard Lake Rd., Suite 20, Farmington Hills, 48018,
>> Robert J. Fund, 626-3366

New York Times, 845 Free Press Bldg., Detroit 48226, John Holusha,
>> 961-7858

Newsweek, 100 Renaissance Center, Detroit 48243, Richard Manning
>> 259-4833

Popular Mechanics, 1302 W. Lafayette Tower, 1321 Orleans, Detroit 48207,
>> Daniel C. Ross, 962-0318

Reuters, 321 Lafayette Blvd., Detroit 48231, John Stark, 961-8371

Time, 1510 Fisher Bldg., West Grand & Second Blvds., Detroit 48202, Paul
      Witterman, 845-1212

U.S. News & World Report, 1120 Free Press Bldg., 321 W. Lafayette St.,
      Detroit 48226, Jack Seamondo, Carey English, 963-6757

United Press International, 945 Free Press Bldg., 321 Lafayette, Detroit
      48226, 965-7950

Wall Street Journal, 333 W. Fort St., Detroit 48226, Doug Sease,
      963-7800

THE FLINT JOURNAL

      200 E. First St., Flint 48502

      (313) 767-0660

State:

      1501 Bank of Lansing Bldg., Lansing 48933

      (517) 487-888, Ed Petykiewicz

      This bureau provides coverage for the Flint Journal and the other
Booth Newspapers of Michigan, which include The Ann Arbor News, Bay City
Times, Grand Rapids Press, Jackson Citizen Patriot, Kalamazoo Chronicle,
Muskegan Chronicle and Saginaw News.

      Booth Newspapers (Box 2168, Grand Rapids 49501) is owned by
Newhouse Newspapers and utilizes the Newhouse News Service. Robert
D. G. Lewis is chief Booth correspondent in the Newhouse bureau at 1750
Pennsylvania Ave., N.W., Wash., D.C. 20006.

THE GRAND RAPIDS PRESS

      Press Plaza, Vandenberg Center, Grand Rapids 49503

      (616) 459-1400

Lansing:

      1501 Bank of Lansing Bldg., Lansing 48933

      (517) 487-8888, Ed Petykiewicz

Washington, D.C.:

      Suite 1320, 1750 Pennsylvania Ave., N.W.

      (202) 383-7800, Robert Fichenberg (Newhouse News Service)

MINNESOTA

MINNEAPOLIS STAR and TRIBUNE

      425 Portland Ave., Minneapolis 55488

      (612) 372-4141

      The Minneapolis Tribune (morning and Sunday) and Minneapolis Star
(evening) merged in 1982 to form an all-day newspaper, one of the largest in
the country. 1983 circulation was 362,000 daily, 358,000 Saturday and
580,000 Sunday, as compared with 1980 daily circulation of the Tribune and

Star of 224,000 and 207,000 respectively and Sunday circulation of 605,000. The Star's Robbinsdale bureau and the Tribune's St. Cloud bureau were closed. The newspaper is a division of Cowles Media Company.

Duluth:
>817 Medical Arts Bldg., Duluth 55802
>(218) 727-7344, Sharon Schmickle

Rochester:
>708 Marquette Bank Bldg., Rochester 55901
>(507) 288-1417, Bill McAuliffe

St. Paul:
>B28B, Press Room, State Capitol, St. Paul 55155
>(612) 222-1673, Lori Sturdevant and Betty Wilson

Washington, D.C.:
>131 F St., N.W., Wash., D.C. 20004
>(202) 347-5885, Finlay Lewis

ST. PAUL DISPATCH
ST. PAUL PIONEER PRESS
>55 E. 4 St., St. Paul 55101
>(612) 222-5011

Washington, D.C.;
>1319 F St., N.W., Wash., D.C. 20004
>(202) 637-3600, Steve Dornfeld (Knight-Ridder)

MISSISSIPPI

THE DAILY HERALD
SOUTH MISSISSIPPI SUN
>Box 4567, Biloxi 39531
>(601) 896-2301
>Biloxi has a population of about 49,000. The success of Gulf

Publishing Company therefore is indicated by these figures—the evening Herald has a circulation of 39,000, the morning Sun has a circulation of 12,000 and the Sun-Herald has a Saturday circulation of 47,000 and a Sunday circulation of 48,000.

Bay St. Louis:
>151 Main St., Bay St. Louis 39520
>(601) 467-6663, Edith B. Back

Jackson:
>Box 2413, Jackson 39205
>(601) 354-8890, Lloyd Gray

Ocean Springs:
>Spring Plaza Shopping Center, Ocean Springs 39563
>(601) 875-2777, Regina Hines

JACKSON CLARION-LEDGER

>Box 40, 311 E. Pearl St., Jackson 39205
>
>(601) 961-7000
>
>The Morning Clarion-Ledger has the largest daily circulation in the state—66,000. On weekends it joins with the evening News to publish the Clarion-Ledger-News—105,000 on Saturday and 116,000 on Sunday.

Biloxi:

>715 Cox Ave., Biloxi 39564
>
>(601) 875-7124, Steve Riley

Greenville:

>1427 Sandy Ave., Greenville 39564
>
>(601) 875-7124, Steve Riley

Starkville:

>203 E. Main St., Starkville 39759
>
>(601) 323-5629, Leigh Hogan

JACKSON DAILY NEWS

>Box 160, 311 E. Pearl St., Jackson 39205
>
>(601) 961-7000
>
>No local bureaus.

MISSOURI

SATURDAY REVIEW

>1205 University Ave., Columbia 65201
>
>(314) 875-3003
>
>The Saturday Review changed ownership and moved from New York in 1982. Mail to its variety of contributing editors and columnists (most are in New York) is channeled via the managing editor, Bruce Van Wyngarder.

THE KANSAS CITY STAR
THE KANSAS CITY TIMES

>1729 Grand Ave., Kansas City 64108
>
>(816) 234-4141
>
>Daily circulation of the morning Times is 285,000, the largest in the state. Circulation of the evening Star is 241,000. Both are owned by the Kansas City Star Co., which also publishes the Sunday Star (circulation 387,000). The newspapers thoroughly cover western Missouri and eastern Kansas with separate bureaus.

THE KANSAS CITY STAR

Missouri

Capitol:

>Box 327, Jefferson City 65101
>
>(314) 634-3565, Jim Sullinger

Clay-Platte Counties:
>> 8123 N. Oak Trafficway, Kansas City 64118
>> (816) 436-4010, Virginia Stollings

Eastern Jackson County:
>> 122 S. Liberty, Independence 64051
>> (816) 254-7744, Mike McGraw

Southern Jackson County:
>> Box 35053, Kansas City 64134
>> (816) 763-0777, John Wylie

Kansas
Johnson City:
>> Box 4129, Overland Park 66204
>> (913) 341-9300, Barry Garron

Wyandotte County:
>> Box 1338, Kansas City 66117
>> (913) 236-8104, Roy Wenzl

Washington, D.C.:
>> 1319 F St., N.W., Wash., D.C. 20004
>> (202) 393-2020, Andrew Miller

THE KANSAS CITY TIMES

Missouri
Capitol:
>> Box 327, Jefferson City 65101
>> (314) 634-3565

Columbia:
>> 1725 Paris Rd., Columbia 65201
>> (314) 449-0514

St. Joseph:
>> 2335 N. Belt Hwy., St. Joseph 64506
>> (816) 364-2800

Kansas
Lawrence:
>> 930 Massachusetts St., Lawrence 66044
>> (913) 842-5701

Washington, D.C.:
>> 1319 F St., N.W., Wash., D.C. 20004
>> (202) 393-2020

ST. LOUIS GLOBE-DEMOCRAT

>> 12th Blvd. at Convention Plaza, St. Louis 63101
>> (314) 342-1212

Jefferson City:

>State Capitol Bldg., Box 628, Jefferson City 65101
>
>(314) 634-3113, Tim Flach

Springfield:

>State Capitol Bldg., Springfield, Ill. 62701
>
>(217) 782-2498, Jim Broadway

Washington, D.C.:

>Suite 1320, 1750 Pennsylvania Ave., N.W., Wash., D.C. 20006
>
>(202) 383-7846, Edward W. O'Brien
>
>(Newhouse News Service)

ST. LOUIS POST-DISPATCH

>900 N. Tucker Blvd., St. Louis 63101
>
>(314) 622-7000
>
>Daily circulation of the evening Post-Dispatch decreased in 1983 to 235,000—slightly behind the morning Globe-Democrat (262,000). Editor and publisher Joseph Pulitzer is heartened a bit on Sundays, when the Post-Dispatch has a circulation of 456,000, the largest in the state, larger than in previous years, and 22nd largest in the country. In 1984, the Post-Dispatch switched to morning publication.

Jefferson City:

>207 Merchants Bank Bldg., Jefferson City 65101
>
>(314) 635-1341, Terry Ganey

Springfield:

>Press Room, Statehouse, Springfield, IL 62706
>
>(217) 525-4912, William Lambrecht

Washington, D.C.:

>1701 Pennsylvania Ave., N.W., Wash., D.C. 20006
>
>(202) 298-6880

ST. LOUIS BUREAUS (area code 314)

Associated Press, Post Dispatch Bldg., 900 N. 12th St., St. Louis
63101, 241-2496

Fairchild Publications, 1040 Paul Brown Bldg., 818 Olive St., St. Louis
63101, 421-0117

United International Press, 900 N. 12th St., St. Louis 63101, 231-6644

Wall Street Journal, 769 Equitable Bldg., 10 Broadway, St. Louis 53102,
John Curley, 471-1904

MONTANA

THE BILLINGS GAZETTE

>Box 2507, 401 Broadway, Billings 59103
>
>(406) 657-1200

The morning Gazette has the state's largest circulation—62,000 daily and 64,000 Sunday.

Bureaus cover a large area in Montana and Wyoming.

Montana

Bozeman:

Box 1532, 812 W. Babcock

(406) 587-4370, William Nell

Glendive:

Box 606, 410 N. Sargent 59330

(406) 365-2761, Sue Saarnio

Helena:

Box 4249, Helena 59601

(406) 443-4920

Wyoming

Cody:

Box 4067F, Rt. 2, Cody 82414

(307) 527-7250, Robert C. Gibson

NEBRASKA

LINCOLN JOURNAL

Box 81689, 926 P St., Lincoln 68501

(402) 473-7231

Washington, D.C.:

3850 Tunlaw Rd., N.W., #212, Wash., D.C. 20007

(202) 244-0241; 965-3372, David E. Lynch

OMAHA WORLD-HERALD

World-Herald Square, Omaha 68102

(402) 444-1000

The morning World-Herald (121,000) and the evening World-Herald (102,000) are the largest circulation newspapers in the state. Sunday circulation is 280,000.

Lincoln:

Suite 1, Executive Bldg., Lincoln 68508

(402) 476-3132, Steven Stingley

Council Bluffs:

210 Park Bldg., Council Bluffs, IO 51501

(712) 322-0079, Gary Newman

Washington, D.C.:

895 Ntl. Press Bldg., Wash., D.C. 20045

(202) 393-0644, Darwin R. Olofson

NEVADA

LAS VEGAS REVIEW JOURNAL
Box 70, Las Vegas 89126
(702) 383-0264
An evening and Sunday newspaper, the Review-Journal has the largest circulation (98,000) in the state, considerably more than its rival, The Las Vegas Sun (52,000).

Carson City:
State Capitol Bldg., Carson City 89710
(702) 885-0788, Chris Broderick

THE NEVADA STATE JOURNAL
THE RENO EVENING GAZETTE
Box 22000, 955 Kuenzli, Reno 89520
(702) 786-8989
Carson City:
Capitol Bldg., Carson City 89701
(702) 882-3553, Lee Adler

NEW HAMPSHIRE

BYTE
70 Main St., Peterborough, NH 03458
(603) 924-9281
San Francisco:
425 Battery St., S.F. 94133
(415) 398-7990, Philip Lemmons
Byte, The Small Systems Journal, is a McGraw-Hill publication and also uses other McGraw-Hill bureaus.

THE UNION LEADER
NEW HAMPSHIRE SUNDAY NEWS
35 Amherst St., Manchester 03105
(603) 668-4321
Largest circulation in the state—67,000 daily and 76,000 Sunday.
Concord:
State House, Concord 03301
(603) 225-3500, Donn Tibbetts
Washington, D.C.:
13514 Duhart Rd., Germantown, MD 20874
(301) 972-4140, Thomas Gorey

NEW JERSEY

ASBURY PARK PRESS
Press Plaza, Asbury Park 07712
(201) 774-7000

The enormous success of the Asbury Park Press is indicated by the following comparison: Asbury Park population—under 20,000. Asbury Park Press circulation—118,000 daily and 167,000 Sunday. The newspaper covers most of central New Jersey, including all of Monmouth and Ocean counties, a growth area. Gary Deckelnick is state editor.

Atlantic City:
Press Rm., City Hall, Atlantic City 08401
(609) 345-2200, Robert McHugh
Brick Township:
1692 Rt. 88, Brick 08723
(202) 458-8220, Joseph Cavaluzzi

Freehold:
29 E. Main St., Freehold 07728
(201) 462-5100, John Hrdzinski
Manahawkin:
300 Rt. 72, Manahawkin 08050
(609) 597-7000, Pete Settles
Red Bank:
15 Monmouth St., Red Bank 07701
(201) 741-5400, Jody Calendar
Toms River:
52 Main St., Toms River 08753
(202) 349-7000, Fred Simmonds
Trenton:
State House, Trenton 08625
(609) 292-5171, Bob De Sando

ATLANTIC CITY PRESS
1900 Atlantic Ave., Atlantic City 08401
(609) 345-1234

Atlantic City has a year-round population of about 41,000 and is located in Atlantic county.

Four-county daily circulation of the morning Press is 79,000; Sunday Press, 85,000.

Brief New Jersey geography lesson. Cape May Court House is the county seat of Cape May county, the southernmost county in New Jersey. It is near, but is not the same as, Cape May, a seashore resort.

Cape May county:

    6 So. Main Street, Cape May Court House 08210, William Watson

    (609) 465-5031

Cumberland county:

    22 W. Landis Avenue, Vineland 08360, Randy Brandt

    (609) 691-8000

Ocean county:

    11 No. Main Street, Manahawkin 08050, Neal Roberts

    (609) 597-1024

Trenton:

    State House, Trenton 08625, Michael Diamond

    (609) 292-4935

Washington, D.C.:

    316 Pennsylvania Avenue, S.E., Washington, D.C. 20003

    (202) 546-7500

COURIER-POST

    Camden 08101

    (609) 663-6000

Trenton:

    118 State House, Trenton 08625

    (609) 292-5052

Washington, D.C.:

    Box 500, Wash., D.C. 20044

    (703) 267-5800 (Gannett News Service)

COMPUTER DEALER

    Box 1952, Dover 07801

    (201) 361-9060

    No bureaus.

THE RECORD

    150 River St., Hackensack 07602

    (201) 646-4000

Trenton:

    Room 119, State House, Trenton 08625

    (609) 292-5159, Peter Yerkes

Wayne:

    36 Preakness Shopping Center, Wayne 07470

    (201) 628-0100, Rodney Allee

Washington, D.C.:

    987 Ntl. Press Bldg., Wash., D.C. 20045

    (202) 638-2127, Robert Cunningham

Formerly called The Bergen Record. The Record now covers Bergen, Hudson and Passaic counties in northern New Jersey and Rockland county, which is one of the growth areas in suburban New York City. Circulation is over 145,000 daily and over 210,000 Sunday.

THE STAR-LEDGER

Star-Ledger Plaza, Court & University Sts., Newark 07101

(201) 877-4141

Daily circulation in 1983 of the morning Star-Ledger was 432,000, largest in the state. Sunday circulation was 632,000, also one of the largest in the country.

Trenton:

State House, Trenton 08625

(609) 292-9280, Leonard Fisher

Washington, D.C.:

1750 Pennsylvania Ave., Wash., D.C. 20006

(202) 383-7823, Robert Cohen (Newhouse News Service)

MEDICAL ECONOMICS

680 Kinderkamack Rd., Oradell 07649

(201) 262-3030

Southeast:

2057 Kansas Ave., N.E., Venetian Isles, St. Petersburg, FL 33703

(813) 522-2803, Philip Harsham

Midwest:

Rm. 450, 20 N. Clark St., Chicago 60602

(312) 368-1770, Rob Cassidy

West Coast:

22835 Islamare Lane, Lake Forest, CA 92630

(714) 768-9129, John E. Carlova

Washington, D.C.:

Suite 902, 200 N. Globe Rd., Arlington, VA 22203

(703) 243-8082, Karen Hunt

THE PRINCETON PACKET

Box 350, 300 Witherspoon St., Princeton 08540

(609) 924-3244

No bureaus.

COMPUTER DECISIONS

50 Essex St., Rochelle Park 07662

(201) 843-0550

Indicative of the growth of the computer industry, Hayden Publishing Company opened bureaus in Silicon Valley, California and near Route 128, Massachusetts.

Hayden Publishing Company also publishes Electronic Design and Microwaves. Its biggest is Computer Decisions, a 119,000-circulation monthly.

California
Southwestern:
    585 W. 29th St., San Pedro 90731
    (213) 548-7877, Jennifer E. Beaver

Northern California:
    1307 S. Mary Ave., Sunnyvale 94087
    (408) 736-6667, Martin Lasden (Western editor), Susan Foster (Microsystems editor).

Midwestern:
    Box 187, Lockport, IL 60441
    (815) 838-5280, Jan Snyders

New England:
    212 Sandwich St., Plymouth, MA 02360
    (617) 746-4441, Mary Mites

TRENTON TIMES

    500 Perry St., Trenton 08605
    (609) 396-3232
    No bureaus.

THE TRENTONIAN

    600 Perry at Southern St., Trenton 08602
    (609) 989-7800

Washington, D.C.:
    654 Pennsylvania Ave., N.E., Wash., D.C. 20003
    (202) 546-9876, John Membrino (States News Service)

THE DISPATCH

    409 39 St., Union City 07087
    (201) 863-2000

Trenton:
    State House, Trenton 08625
    (609) 292-2121, Dan Akst

TRENTON BUREAUS (area code 609)

Asbury Park Press, State House, Trenton 08625, Bob De Sando, 292-5171

Associated Press, State House, Trenton 08625, 292-5176

Atlantic City Press, State House, Trenton 08625, Michael Diamond, 292-4935

Camden Courier-Post, 118 State House, Trenton 08625, 292-5052

Hackensack Record, 119 State House, Trenton 08625, 292-5159

New York Times, Press Rm., State House, W. State St., Trenton 08625, Joe Sullivan, 292-2121

Newark Star-Ledger, State House, Trenton 08625, Leonard Fisher, 292-9280, Peter Yerkes, 292-5151

Philadelphia Inquirer, 206 W. State St., Trenton 08608, Tracy McCrary, John Hilferty, 989-8990

Union City Dispatch, State House, Trenton 08625, Dan Akst, 292-2121

United Press International, 500 Perry St., Trenton Times Bldg., Trenton 06805, 392-0700

NEW MEXICO

ALBUQUERQUE JOURNAL

P.O. Drawer J, 7th and Silver, S.W., Albuquerque 87103

(505) 842-2300

The morning Journal has the state's largest circulation (91,000 daily, 131,000 Sunday). The evening Tribune (a Scripps-Howard newspaper), has the second largest circulation (45,000) of the state's 20 dailies.

Both obtained circulation highs in 1983.

Las Cruces:

206 S. Main St., Las Cruces 88001

(505) 526-4461, Joe Smith

Santa Fe:

Box 1534, 320 Galisteo, Santa Fe 87501

(505) 988-8881, David Steinberg, Larry Calloway

Washington, D.C.:

3267 P St., N.W., Wash., D.C. 20007

(202) 338-2240, Paul Wieck

ALBUQUERQUE TRIBUNE

P.O. Drawer T, 717 Silver Ave., S.W., Albuquerque 87103

(505) 842-2300

Washington, D.C.:

1110 Vermont Ave., N.W., Wash., D.C. 20005

(202) 347-7750, Jerry Conto (Scripps-Howard)

NEW YORK

THE TIMES-UNION
THE KNICKERBOCKER NEWS

645 Albany-Shaker Rd., Albany 12212

(518) 454-5411

Though these newspapers cover northeastern New York and parts of Vermont and Massachusetts with several editions, the entire editorial staff is headquartered in Albany and the only full-time bureau is the Hearst bureau in Washington, D.C.:

1701 Pennsylvania Ave., N.W., Wash., D.C. 20006

(202) 298-6920, Joseph Kingsbury Smith

ALBANY BUREAUS (area code 518)

The Legislative Correspondents Association maintains a Press Room in the Legislative Office Building and in the State Capitol. The Association address is Box 7135, Albany 12224. Members of the Association represent the following media, on a full or part-time basis:

Albany Knickerbocker News and Times Union

American Banker

Associated Press

Buffalo News

Gannett News Service

Gannett-Westchester Newspapers

Journal of Commerce

Middletown Times-Herald

Newsday

New York Daily News

New York Post

New York Times

Schenectady Gazette

Syracuse Herald Journal and Post Standard

Staten Island Advance

Troy Times Record

United Press

Watertown Times

Following are the major bureaus:

Associated Press, Capital Newspapers Bldg., 645 Shaker Rd., Albany 12211,
488-7821

Buffalo News, Box 7262, State Capitol, Albany 12224, Dave Ernst,
434-6365

New York Post, State Capitol, Albany 12224, Fred Dicker, 465-9623

New York Times, State Capitol, Albany 12224, Michael Oreshes,
436-0757

Newsday, Box 7255, Albany 12224, 465-2311

Schenectady Gazette, State Capitol, Albany 12055, Bob Groneman, 462-2499

Schenectady Gazette, Wellington Hotel, State St., Albany,12055, Steve
Nelson, 434-2912

United Press International, 645 Albany Shaker Rd., Albany 12221,
458-7833

BUFFALO NEWS

1 News Plaza, Buffalo 14240

((716) 849-4444

With the demise of the Buffalo Courier Express, the Buffalo News
(formerly the Buffalo Evening News) now is an all-day newspaper.

Albany:

Box 7262, State CApitol, Albany 12224

(518) 434-6365, Dave Ernst

Amherst:

Amherst Town Hall, Williamsville 14221

(716) 632-2676, Richard Dawson

Cheektowaga:

Union Rd., Cheektowaga Central High School, Cheektowaga 14225

(716) 681-4516, Kim Lukasiak

Niagara Falls:

9701 Pine Ave., Niagara Falls 14304

(716) 397-9304, Dick Baldwin

Olean:

Box 134, Olean 14760

(716) 372-8375, Bert Freed

Tonawanda:

Box 89, 3491 Delaware Ave., Kenore 14217

(716) 873-1333, Bob Dearing

West Seneca:

3976 Seneca St., West Seneca 14224

(716) 674-9393, Dave Condren

Washington, D.C.:

1284 Ntl. Press Bldg. Wash., D.C. 20045

(202) 737-3188, Richard D. McCarthy

NEW YORK CITY

AMERICAN BANKER
1 State Street Plaza, N.Y. 10004
(212) 943-6700

Chicago:
53 W. Jackson Blvd., Chicago 60604
(312) 427-4347

San Francisco:
235 Montgomery St., San Francisco 94104
(415) 362-1472, Geoff Brouillette

Washington D.C.:
1180 Natl. Press Bldg., Wash., D.C. 20045
(202) 347-5529, Robert Trigaux

THE ASSOCIATED PRESS
50 Rockefeller Plaza, N.Y. 10020
(212) 262-4000

The A.P. maintains bureaus and offices in all major cities, ranging from one person at a desk within a newspaper office to its bureau in our nation's capital with a staff of more than a hundred people. Publicists are cautioned not to mail identical news releases to several bureaus. Following is a list of all domestic bureaus. Publicists are urged to respect the importance of this list. *Do not send identical releases to more than one bureau.* Do not send trade news, local items or other material of interest only to a single publication.

In 1983, The ASsociated Press reported 1,316 daily newspapers and ;5,700 broadcast members in the U.S., considerably more than United Press, particularly among radio stations.

The following list includes all domestic bureaus.

Alabama:
News Bldg., Fourth Ave., and 22 St., N., Birmingham 35203
(205) 251-4221
304 Government St., Mobile 36601
(205) 433-7269
Alabama Jnl. Bldg., S. Lawrence St., Montgomery 36101
(205) 262-5947

Alaska:
Box 2175, Anchorage 99502
(907) 272-1131

State Capitol, Juneau 99801
(907) 586-1515

Arizona:

Republic & Gazette Bldg., 120 E. Van Buren St., Phoenix 85004

(602) 258-8934

Box 26807, Tucson 85726

(602) 294-1440

Arkansas:

1101 W. Second Ave., Little Rock 7220

(501) 374-5536

California:

1626 E. St., Fresno 93786

(209) 264-3000

1111 S. Hil St., Los Angeles 90015

(213) 746-1200

927 L St., Sacramento 95814

(916) 448-9555

Union-Tribune Bldg., San Diego 92112

(619) 231-3587

318 Fox Plaza, San Francisco 94119

(415) 621-7432, Martin C. Thompson

Colorado:

650 Fifteenth St., Denver 80202

(303) 825-0123, Joe A. McGowan, Jr.

Connecticut:

241 Asylum Ave., Hartford 06103

(203) 246-6876

40 Sargent Dr., New Haven 06519

(203) 624-9825

Delaware:

Box 934, State Capitol, Dover 19901

(302) 674-3037

District of Columbia:

2021 K St., N.W., Wash., D.C. 20006

(202) 833-5300, Walter Mears

Florida:

One Riverside Ave., Jacksonville 32202

(904) 356-2829

I.B.M. Building, 2125 Biscayne Blvd., Miami 33137

(305) 573-7230,

633 N. Orange Ave., Orlando 32801

(305) 425-4547

306 S. Duval St., Tallahassee 32304

(904) 224-1211

Box 2972, Tampa Tribune Bldg., Tampa 33601

(813) 223-3270

Georgia:
>
> 500 S. Omni International, Atlanta 30335
> (404) 522-8971, Carl Bell

Hawaii:
>
> Box 2956, Hawaii Newspaper Agency News Bldg., Honolulu 96802
> (808) 536-5510, Ron Staton

Idaho:
>
> 419 State Capitol, Boise 83701
> (208) 376-1894

Illinois:
>
> Evening Sentinel Bldg., Centralia 62801
> (618) 533-2259
> 230 N. Michigan Ave., Chicago 60601
> (312) 781-0500, Thomas Dygard
> Journal Star Bldg., War Memorial Dr., Peoria 61601
> (309) 682-0141
> Press Room, State Capitol, Springfield 62704
> (217) 789-2700

Indiana:
>
> Star-News Bldg., 307 N. Pennsylvania St., Indianapolis 46204
> (317) 639-5501
> 223 W. Colfax, South Bend 46626
> (219) 228-1649

Iowa:
>
> Box 1741, 715 Locust, Des Moines 50306
> (515) 243-3281

Kansas:
>
> 616 Jefferson St., Topeka 66607
> (913) 234-5654
> 825 E. Douglas, Wichita 67201
> (316) 263-4601

Kentucky:
>
> State CApitol, Frankfort 40601
> (502) 223-3222
> Herald Leader Bldg., Main & Midland, Lexington 40507
> (606) 254-2070
> 407-A Courier-Jnl. & Times Bldg., Louisville 40204
> (502) 583-7718

Louisiana:
>
> Box 44395, State Capitaol Bldg., Baton Rouge 70821
> (504) 343-1325
> Times-Picayune-States Bldg., 1001 Howard Ave., Suite 2000A, New
>   Orleans 70140
> (504) 821-3931

Maine:

Box 1471, State House, Augusta 04330
(207) 289-2671
Press Herald Bldg., 390 Congress St., Portland 04104
(207) 772-4157

Maryland:

State House, State Circle, Annapolis 21404
(301) 269-0196
222 St. Paul Pl., Baltimore 21202
(301) 539-3524
100 Summit Ave.,-Hagerstown 21740
(301) 791-5246

Massachusetts:

184 High St., Boston 02110
(617) 357-8100,
115 State St., Springfield 01103
(413) 781-0217

Michigan:

660 Plaza Dr., Suite 2000, Detroit 48226
(313) 965-9500
Press Bldg., 115 Michigan, N.W., Grand Rapids 49503
(616) 458-8853
1112 Bank of Lansing Bldg., Lansing 48933
(517) 482-8011

Minnesota:

426 Portland Ave., South, Minneapolis 53415-1585
(612) 332-2724
200 State Capitol Bldg., St. Paul 55155
(612) 296-6561

Mississippi:

Box 446, Jackson 39205
(601) 948-5897, 353-2421

Missouri:

Box 272, Jefferson City 65101
(314) 636-9415
Star Bldg., 1715 Grand Ave., Kansas City 64108-1850
(816) 421-4844
Post-Dispatch Bldg., 900 N. 12 St., St. Louis 63101
(314) 241!2496

Montana:

Box 5810, Independent Record Bldg., Helena 59604-5810
(406) 442-7440

Nebraska:
>Box 82061, Lincoln 68508
>(402) 432-2525
>Box 838, Downtown Station, Omaha 68101-0838
>(402) 341-4963

Nevada:
>State Capitol, Carson City 89701
>(702) 885-4190
>Review-Journal Bldg., Las Vegas 89101
>(702) 382-7440
>Gazette-Journal Bldg., Reno 89504
>(702) 322-3639

New Hampshire:
>The Monitor Bldg., Concord 03301-1296
>(603) 225-3327

New Jersey:
>c/o The Press, Devins Lane, Pleasantville 08232
>(609) 645-2063
>Airport Int'l Plaza, Routes 1 & 9 South, Newark 07114
>(201) 596-0296
>State House, Trenton 08625
>(609) 292-5176

New Mexico:
>Tribune Bldg., Albuquerque 87103
>(505) 243-785
>Press Room, State Capitol, Santa Fe 87501
>(505) 982-1012

New York:
>Capital-Newspapers Bldg., 645 Albany-Shaker Rd., Albany 12211
>(518) 458-7821
>News Bldg., 1 News Plaza, Buffalo 14240
>(716) 852-1051
>Room 137, State Supreme Court Bldg., Mineola 11501
>(516) 746-3484
>50 Rockefeller Plaza, New York 10020
>(212) 262-4000
>Secretariat Bldg., United Nations, New York 10017
>(212) 262-6227
>Syracuse Herald-Journal, Clinton Sq., Syracuse 13201
>(315) 471-6471
>Press Rm., County Bldg., 148 Martine Ave., White Plains 10601
>(914) 946-8841

North Carolina:

    Box 2138, Charlotte 28201

    (704) 334-4624

    219 McDowell St., Raleigh 27602

    (919) 833-8687

North Dakota:

    Box 1018, Bismarck 58501

    (701) 223-8450

    Forum Bldg., Fargo 58103

    (701) 235-1908

Ohio:

    Box 206, Enquirer Bldg., 617 Vine St., Cincinnati 45202

    (513) 241-2386

    Cleveland Plaza Hotel, 1127 Euclid Ave., Cleveland 44114

    (216) 771-2172

    Dispatch Bldg., 34 S. Third St., Columbus 43215

    (614) 228-4306, William DiMascio

Oklahoma:

    Old Daily Oklahoman Bldg., 500 N. B'way., Oklahoma City 73102

    (405) 236-0663

    315 S. Boulder, Tulsa 74103

    (918) 584-4346

Oregon:

    Box 1468, Grants Pass 97526

    (503) 476-1722

    1320 S.W. B'way, Portland 97201

    (503) 228-2169

    Press Room, State Capitol, Salem 97310

    (503) 363-0010

Pennsylvania:

    508 Payne-Shoemaker Bldg., 240 N. Third St., Harrisburg 17101

    (717) 238-9413

    Box 7784, Philadelphia 19101

    (215) 382-5571, George L. Zucker

    1111 Clark Bldg., 717 Liberty Ave., Pittsburgh 15222

    (412) 281-3747

Rhode Island:

    10 Dorrance St., Providence 02903

    (401) 274-2270

South Carolina:

    State and Record Bldg., Stadium Rd., Columbia 29202

    (803) 771-6161

South Dakota:
>
> Box 368, Capitol Bldg., Pierre 57501
> (605) 224-7811
> Argus-Leader Bldg., Sioux Falls 57101
> (605) 332-3111

Tennessee:
>
> 400 E. 11th St., Chattanooga 37402
> (615) 266-4600
> 204 W. Church St., News Sentinel Bldg., Knoxville 37901
> (615) 522-3963
> Press-Scimitar and Commercial Appeal Bldg., 495 Union Ave.,
> Memphis 38101
> (901) 525-1972
> Banner-Tennessean Bldg., 1100 B'way, Nashville 37202
> (615) 244-2205

Texas:
>
> Box 12247, Capitol Station, State Capitol, Austin 78711
> (512) 472-4004
> Southland Center, Suite 2100, Dallas 75201
> (214) 742-3447
> Fort Worth Star-Telegram Bldg., Fort Worth 76101
> (817) 336-9271
> KGBT Bldg., Harlingen 78550
> (512) 423-7790
> 609 Fannin St., Houston 77002
> (713) 236-8181
> Ave. E & 3rd St., San Antonio 78206
> (512) 222-2713

Utah:
>
> Rm 323, Annex, 143 S. Main St., Salt Lake City 84111
> (801) 322-3405

Vermont:
>
> Thrush Tavern, 107 Main St., Montpelier 05602
> (802) 223-7638

Virginia:
>
> 150 Brambleton Ave., Norfolk 23510
> (703) 625-2047
> Box 27603, Richmond 23261
> (703) 643-6646

Washington:
>
> Box 607, Legislative Bldg., Olympia 98501
> (206) 753-7222
> 201 Boren North, Seattle 98111
> (206) 682-1812

Box 2173, Spokane 99210

(509) 624-1258

West Virginia:

Gazette & Mail Bldg., 1001 Virginia St E., Charleston 25326

(304) 346-0897

Huntington Pub. Co., Huntington 25709

(304) 523-8721

Wisconsin:

1901 Fish Hatchery Rd., Madison 53701

(608) 252-6297

Journal Sq., 922 N. Fourth St., Milwaukee 53203

(414) 271-0158

Wyoming:

115 E. 22 St., Wyo. Educ. Assoc. Bldg., Cheyenne 82001

(307) 632-9351

In addition to its prolific news coverage, The Associated Press distributes, by mail and wire, a variety of by-lined columns and features. The New York bureau includes, for example. George Cornell (religion) and many others. Cecily Brownstone does her food column from her Greenwich Village home at 81 Jane St., N.Y. 10014.

In many cases, mail delivery is expedited, particularly on weekends and holidays, by using post office box numbers instead of street addresses.

Following are the p.o. box numbers of many of the A.P. offices (listed alphabetically, by state):

Tucson—26807	Albany—11010
Los Angeles—54247	Charlotte—2138
San Francisco—7247	Raleigh—1311
Hartford—3437	Bismarck—1018
Dover—934	Cincinnati—206
Tampa—2972	Columbus—1812
Honolulu—2956	Tulsa—1770
Boise—327	Philadelphia—7784
Des Moines—1741	Columbia—1435
Baton Rouge—44395	Pierre—368
Portland—617	Sioux Falls—1125
Annapolis—1471	Memphis—326
Jackson—446	Nashville—22990
Jefferson City—272	Austin—12247
Helena—5810	Richmond—22603
Lincoln—82061	Olympia—607
Omaha—838	Seattle—2144
Reno—22000	Spokane—2173
Concord—1296	Charleston—1713
Albuquerque—1845	Huntington—445
Santa Fe—2326	Cheyenne—1323

Following are the A.P. "control bureaus," which function as regional headquarters:

Albany	Concord, NH
Albuquerque	Dallas
Atlanta	Denver
Baltimore	Des Moines
Boston	Detroit
Charleston, WV	Hartford
Chicago	Kansas City, MO
Columbus, OH	Los Angeles
Miami	Philadelphia
Milwaukee	Phoenix
Minneapolis	Raleigh
Nashville	Richmond
New Orleans	Salt Lake City
New York	San Francisco
Neward	Seattle
Oklahoma City	

REMINDER: Do not mass mail news releases to more than one bureau!

AVIATION WEEK & SPACE TECHNOLOGY

1221 Ave. of the Americas, N.Y. 10020

(212) 512-2000

Dallas:

5151 Beltline Rd., Dallas 75240

(214) 458-2400, Irwin Bulban

Los Angeles:

3333 Wilshire Blvd., L.A. 90010

(213) 478-1160, Robert R. Ropelewski

San Franciso:

425 Battery St., San Francisco 94111

(415) 362-4600, Richard G. O'Lone

southeast:

Box H, Cocoa Beach, FL 32931

(305) 783-7997, Harry Kolcum

Washington, D.C.:

1777 N. Kent St., Arlington VA 22209

(202) 463-1770, Herbert Coleman, William Gregory

BACK STAGE

312 W. 42 St., N.Y. 10036

(212) 947-0200

Chicago:

    841 N. Addison Ave., Elmhurst 60126

    (31q) 834-7533, Wil Anderson

Los Angeles;:

    5670 Wilshire Blvd., L.A. 90036

    (213) 936-5200, Bob Harris

BARRON'S WEEKLY

    22 Cortland St., N.Y. 10007

    (212) 285-5000

    Barron's is published by Down Jones & Company, which also publishes The Wall Street Journal. Barron's has its own news staff in Washington, D.C., but editor Robert Bleiberg prefers to have all material sent to the New York office.

BILLBOARD

1515 Broadway, N.Y. 10036

(212) 764-7300

Cincinnati:

    2160 Patterson St., Cincinnati 45214

    (513) 381-6450

Los Angeles:

    9107 Wilshire Blvd., Beverly Hills 90210

    (213) 273-7040, Lee Zhito, Sam Sutherland

Nashville:

    14 Music Circle E., Nashville 37203

    (615) 748-8100, Kip Kirby

Washington, D.C.:

    733 15th St., N.W., Wash., D.C. 20005

    (202) 783-3282, Bill Holland

    "The international news weekly of music and Home entertainment", Billboard moved its headquarters from Los Angeles to New York and closed its Chicago bureau. The Cincinnati bureau is for its directories.

THE BOND BUYER

    One State Street Plaza, N.Y. 10004

    (212) 943-8200

Washington, D.C.:

    529 Fourteenth St., N.W., Wash., D.C. 20045

    (202) 293-4727, Craig Ferris

    Also publishes American Banker, Daily Bond Buyer, Money Manager and Weekly Bond Buyer.

BUSINESS WEEK

1221 Ave. of the Americas, N.Y. 10020

(212) 512-2000

Circulation of this weekly news magazine is 776,000. A few of the bureaus cover specific industries, including automobiles (Detroit), rubber (Cleveland), energy (Houston) and metals (Pittsburgh). The industrial edition of Business Week has special correspondents—Larry Armstrong in Chicago and David Cook in Detroit. Maryanne McNellis in the Los Angeles bureau covers the Pacific Basin (including Hawaii and Australia). A Connecticut bureau was opened in 1980.

Atlanta:

4170 Ashford-Dunwoody Rd., Atlanta 30319

(404) 252-0626, Tony Heffernan

Boston:

McGraw-Hill Bldg., Copley Sq., Boston 02116

(617) 262-1160, Emily Smith

Chicago:

645 N. Michigan Ave., Chicago 60611

(312) 751-3813, Mark Morrison

Cleveland:

55 Public Square, Cleveland 44113

(216) 781-7000

Connecticut:

47 Wellsweep Dr., Madison 06443

(203) 245-1620, Resa W. King

Dallas:

2001 Bryan Tower, Dallas 75201

(214) 742-1747, Michael Sheldrick

Denver:

655 Broadway, Denver 80203

(303) 825-6731, Sandra Atchison

Detroit:

3756 City Nat'l Bank Bldg., Detroit 48226

(313) 962-5600, William Hampton

Houston:

375 Dresser Tower, Houston 77002

(713) 659-1692, James Norman

Los Angeles:

3200 Wilshire Blvd., L.A. 90010

(213) 487-1160, Stewart Toy

Minneapolis-St. Paul:

    730 Second Ave., Minneapolis 55402

    (612) 332-8577, Thane Peterson

Pacific Basin (Hawaii, Australia):

    3200 Wilshire Blvd., L.A. 90010

    (213) 487-1160, Maryanne McNellis

Philadelphia:

    3 Parkway, Philadelphia 19102

    (215) 568-6161, Robin Carlson

Pittsburgh:

    6 Gateway Center, Pittsburgh 15222

    (412) 227-3640, William Symonds

San Francisco:

    425 Battery St., San Francisco 94111

    (415) 362-4600, Herbert Lawson

Washington, D.C.:

    400 Ntl. Press Bldg., Wash., D.C. 20045

    (202) 737-6630, Robert E. Farrell

    The Washington Bureau, with a staff of 27, serves all of the McGraw-Hill publications. Keith Felcyn, in New York, is chief of correspondents of Business Week.

CABLE MARKETING

    352 Park Ave., S., N.Y. 10010

    (212) 685-4848

    Established in 1980, Cable Marketing is published monthly by a division of Jobson Publishing Corp. Circulation is about 15,000.

CASH BOX

    1775 Broadway, Suite 630, N.Y. 10019

    (212) 586-2640

Chicago:

    29 E. Madison St., Chicago 60602

    (312) 346-7272, Camille Compasio (vending)

Los Angeles:

    6363 Sunset Blvd., Hollywood 90028

    (213) 464-8241, Richard Imamuro

Nashville:

    21 Music Circle East, Nashville 37203

    (615) 244-2898, Jim Sharp

Washington, D.C.:

    3518 N. Utah St., Arlington, Va. 22207

    (703) 243-5664, Earl B. Abrams

CHAIN STORE AGE

425 Park Ave., N.Y. 10022

(212) 371-9400

Los Angeles:

606 N. Larchmont Blvd., L.A. 90004

(213) 464-8321, John Donoghue

Washington, D.C.:

177-35 Striley Dr., Wash., D.C. 20861

(301) 774-3895, Kenneth Rankin

A Lebhar-Friedman monthly publication. The same bureaus are used for the company's other publications, Discount Store News, Drug Store News, Inside Retailing, Nation's Restaurant News, National Home Center News and General Merchandise.

CHEMICAL WEEK

1221 Avenue of the Americas, N.Y. 10020

(212) 512-2000

In each McGraw-Hill bureau, a person is assigned to the chemical beat, as follows:

Atlanta:

610 Gas Light Tower, 235 Peachtree St. N.E., Atlanta 30309

(404) 521-3287, Inge Kummant

Chicago:

645 N. Michigan Ave., Chicago 60611

(312) 751-3700, Jeff Ryser

Dallas:

907 Preston Wood Towers, 5151 Beltline Rd., Dallas 75240

(214) 458-2400, Lorraine Smith

Detroit:

3756 City National Bank Bldg., Detroit 48226

(313) 962-5600, David Whiteside, James Schwartz

Houston:

375 Dresser Tower, 601 Jefferson St., Houston 77002

(713) 659-4558, Eric Johnson

San Francisco:

425 Battery St., San Francisco 94111

(415) 362-4600, Margaret Ralston Drossel, Jenness Keene

Washington, D.C.:

1120 Vermont Ave., N.W., Wash., D.C. 20045

(202) 463-1600, Robert E. Farrell

COMMERCIAL & FINANCIAL CHRONICLE

120 Broadway, N.Y. 10271

(212) 344-4242, John Dunne

Boston:

4 Water St., Arlington 02174

(617) 643-7900, C. Peter Jorgensen

CONVENIENCE STORE NEWS

254 W. 31 St., N.Y. 10001

(212) 594-4120

No bureaus. BMT Publications also publishes Gaming Business
Magazine Smokeshop and United States Tobacco and Candy Journal.

DATAMATION

875 Third Ave., N.Y. 10022

(212) 605-9400

Boston:

1 Chaucer Road, RFD #2, Sandwich 02563

(617) 888-6312, Ralph Emmett

Los Angeles:

1801 S. La Cienega Blvd., L.A. 90035

(213) 559-5111, Edith Myers

San Francisco Area:

2680 Bayshore Frontage Rd., Mountain View 94043

(415) 965-8222, Ed Yasaki

DUN'S BUSINESS MONTH

875 Third Ave., N.Y. 10022

(212) 605-9400

Dun & Bradstreet has many offices but its magazine, Dun's Business
Month (formerly Dun's Review) maintains only three U.S. bureaus.

Chicago:

303 E. Wacker Dr., Chic. 60601

(312) 938-2935, Lynn Atkins

Washington D.C.:

912 S. 26 Pl., Arlington, VA 22202

(703) 549-0881, Marilyn Wilson

West Coast:

3042 Country Club Drive, Costa Mesa 92626

(714) 540-5518, Thomas J. Murray

Dun-Donnelly Publishing Corp. includes a large number of trade and
professional publications which do not maintain bureaus. The group includes:
Graphic Arts Monthly, Cutis, Furniture Design & Manufacturing, Fire
Engineering, Roads & Streets, Water & Wastes Engineering, Control
Engineering, Industrial Research, World Construction, American Journal of
Medicine and American Journal of Surgery. The TravelAge publications do
maintain bureaus and are listed separately.

EDITOR & PUBLISHER

575 Lexington Ave., N.Y. 10022

(212) 752-7050

Chicago:

303 E. Ohio St., Chicago 60611

(312) 565-0123, Mark Fitzgerald

Washington, D.C.:

1295 Ntl. Press Bldg., Wash., D.C. 20045

(202) 628-8365, James E. Roher

ELECTRICAL WORLD

1221 Ave. of the Americas, N.Y. 10020

(212) 512-2000

No bureaus.

ELECTRONICS

1221 Avenue of the Americas, N.Y. 10020

(212) 512-2000

Published biweekly by McGraw-Hill, Electronics is a major influence in the engineering field (circulation: over 100,000). Editor-in-Chief Samuel Weber supervises a large staff of editors and bureaus.

Boston:

McGraw-Hill Bldg., 607 Boyston St., Boston 02116

(617) 262-1160, Linda Lowe, Norman Alster

Chicago:

645 N. Michigan Ave., Chicago 60611

(312) 751-3824, Wesley Iverson

Dallas:

2001 Bryan Tower, Dallas 75201

(214) 458-2400, J. Robert Lineback

Los Angeles:

3200 Wilshire Blvd., South Tower, L.A. 90010

(213) 487-1160, Larry Waller

Palo Alto:

1000 Elwell Court, Palo Alto, Ca. 94903

(415) 968-2712, Clifford Barney, Stephen Fields

Washington, D.C.:

433 Ntl. Press Bldg., Wash., D.C. 20045

(202) 462-1650, Ray Connolly, Karen Berney

ESQUIRE

2 Park Ave., N.Y. 10016

(212) 561-8100

Washington, D.C.:

3748 Huntington St., N.W., Wash., D.C. 20015

(202) 362-9040, Jerrold Schecter

ESSENCE

1500 Broadway, New York 10036

(212) 730-4260

Circulation 750,000, a monthly service magazine for black women.
No bureaus.

FAIRCHILD PUBLICATIONS

7 E. 12 St., N.Y. 10003

(212) 741-4000 (after 5 p.m., 741-4360)

The Fairchild building in New York houses several of the largest and most influential editorial staffs of any trade or business publication. The bureaus are more important with Fairchild than with most other publishers, and releases should be sent to the Fairchild bureau nearest to the company or news source. Fairchild editors generally prefer to check information with the company or industry spokesman, rather than public relations intermediaries, and they are extremely thorough in covering their territories.

The Fairchild Consumer and Trade publications in New York are:

American Metal Market

DNR—Daily News Record

Electronic News

Electronic Retailing

Energy User News

Entree

Footwear News

HFD-Retailing Home Furnishings

Heat Treating

Home Fashions Textiles

Inside Furniture

M

Men's Wear

Metal Center News

Metalworking News

MIS Week

Multichannel News

Sportstyle

Supermarket News

W

WWD-Women's Wear Daily

In addition, Fairchild also has three other groups, which have separate staffs and are headquartered elsewhere.

International Medical News Group
Aches & Pains
Clinical Psychiatry News
Family Practice News
Internal Medicine News
Ob. Gyn. News
Pediatric News
Skin & Allergy News

Professional Press Inc.
International Contact Lens Clinic
The Journal of Learning Disabilities
Optometric Monthly
Optical Index

American Traveler Group
El Travel Agent Internacional
Interline Reporter
Travel Agent

Fairchild Publications is a Capital Cities Communications Company, which also publishes many daily and weekly newspapers, including the Kansas City Star/Times, Red Bank (NJ) Daily Register, Wilkes-Barre Times Leader and Fort Worth Star-Telegram.

Following are the Fairchild bureaus:

Atlanta:

57 Executive Park So., Suite 380, Atlanta 30329
(404) 633-9253

Boston:

480 Boylston St., Boston 02116
(617) 267-8282

Charlotte:

Park 77 Office Bldg., 500 Archdale Dr., Charlotte 28210
(704) 525-6724, Ray Chune

Chicago:

11 E. Adams St., Chicago 60603
(312) 663-3500, Ann Keeton (men's) Maria Paul (women's)

Cincinnati:

1615 Carew Tower, Cincinnati 45202
(513) 721-7464

Cleveland:

Citizens Federal Tower, 2000 E. 9th St., Cleveland 44115
(216) 241-5940

Dallas:

2730 Stemmons Fwy., Dallas 75207
(214) 630-5461, Nina Flournay

Denver:
  1762 Emerson St., Denver 80218
  (303) 832-4141
Detroit:
  New Center Bldg., Detroit 48202
  (313) 871-7150
Greenville:
  Box 16165, Station B, SC 29606
  (803) 233-6946
High Point:
  210 Commerce St., High Point, NC 27260
  (919) 885-2296
Houston:
  Suite 853, 801 Texas Ave., Houston 77002
  (713) 223-0194
Los Angeles:
  615 So. Flower St., L.A. 90011
  (213) 624-1981, Steve Ginsberg
Miami:
  1100 NE 125 St., No. Miami 33161
  (305) 895-6111
Minneapolis:
  920 Nicollet Mall, Minneapolis 55402
  (612) 339-0697
Philadelphia:
  WPVI-TV Bldg., 4100 City Line Ave., Philadelphia 19131
  (412) 566-1260
St. Louis:
  1040 Paul Brown Bldg., 818 Olive St., St. Louis 63103
  (314) 421-0117
San Francisco:
  760 Market St., San Francisco 94102
  (415) 781-8921
Washington, D.C.:
  1333 H. St., N.W., Wash., D.C. 20045
  (202) 682-3200, Lloyd Schwartz

FAMILY WEEKLY

  1515 Broadway, N.Y. 10036
  (212) 719-6900
  Family Weekly is a weekend supplement distributed in over 360
newspapers, with a circulation of 12,500,000!
  No bureaus.

FIELD AND STREAM

1515 Broadway, N.Y. 10036

(212) 719-6900

Circulation two million. A CBS monthly magazine. Mail is forwarded to the regional editors, Jerry Myers (South), John Spehn (Midwest) and Tom Opre (Central).

FINANCIAL WORLD

1250 Broadway, N.Y. 10001

(212) 244-5500

This semi-monthly magazine, of which Kermit Lansner is editor-in-chief, does not maintain bureaus.

FORBES

60 Fifth Ave., N.Y. 10011

(212) 620-2200

Circulation of this influential biweekly magazine now is over 700,000

Midwestern:

1064 Wrigley Bldg., 410 N. Michigan Ave., Chicago 60611

(312) 329-1562, Jill Bettner

Southwestern:

2 Shell Plaza Bldg., Houston 77002

(713) 228-2800, William Baldwin

Los Angeles:

12233 W. Olympia Blvd., L.A. 90064

(213) 628-2344, Laury Minard

Washington, D.C.:

399 Ntl. Press Bldg., Wash., D.C. 20045,

(202) 628-2344, Jerry Flint

FORTUNE

1271 Avenue of the Americas, N.Y. 10020

(212) 586-1212

The change, early in 1978, from monthly to semi-monthly, and the new emphasis on shorter news-oriented articles has resulted in an increase in the Fortune staff, including correspondents located in the Time bureaus in three cities. New York contacts are Ann Hengstenberg and Alan Demaree.

Houston:

914 Main St., Houston 77002

(713) 759-9499, Alexander Stuart

California:

Suite 150, 1333 Lawrence Expressway, Santa Clara 95051

(408) 246-1403, Gary Hector

Washington, D.C.:
>919 18 St., N.W., Wash., D.C. 20006
>
>(202) 429-9620, Paul Weaver

GRALLA PUBLICATIONS

>1515 Broadway, N.Y. 10036
>
>(212) 869-1300
>
>Magazines of Gralla Publications include Bank Systems & Equipment, Catalog Showroom Business, Contract, Facilities Design and Management, Giftware Business, Health Care Systems, Impressions, Kitchen Business, Meeting News, Merchandising, MultiHousing News, National Jeweler, Premium Indentive Business, Sporting Goods Business, Travel Agents Marketplace. All are published in New York, except Impressions, which is published at the Dallas office.

Chicago:
>3525 W. Peterson Ave., Chicago 60659
>
>(312) 463-1102

Dallas:
>15400 Knoll Trail Dr., Dallas 75248
>
>(214) 239-3060

Los Angeles:
>16200 Ventura Blvd., Encino, CA 91438
>
>(213) 788-0271

HARPER'S BAZAAR MAGAZINE

>1700 Broadway, N.Y. 10019
>
>(212) 903-5000

California:
>3420 Ocean Park Blvd., Santa Monica 90405
>
>(213) 462-6788, Mrs. Nancy Dinsmore
>
>Sent all editorial material to N.Y.

THE HEARST CORPORATION

>959 Eighth Ave., N.Y. 10019
>
>(212) 262-5700

Washington, D.C.:
>1701 Pennsylvania Ave., N.W., Wash., D.C. 20006
>
>(202) 298-6920, Joseph Kingsbury-Smith, national editor; Robert Thompsen, bureau chief.
>
>The Hearst magazines headquartered at 224 W. 57 St., N.Y. 10019, phone (212) 262-5700, are American Druggist, Colonial Homes, Connoisseur, Cosmopolitan, Country Living, Good Housekeeping and Sports Afield—which do not have bureaus—plus Motor Magazine, Motor Boating & Sailing, Popular Mechanics, Redbook. The bureaus for these publications are listed separately.

The Hearst magazines headquartered at 1700 Broadway, N.Y. 10019, phone (212) 903-5000 are Harper's Bazaar, House Beautiful and Town & Country. Science Digest is at 888 Seventh Ave., N.Y. 10106.

The Hearst Corp. newspapers are:

The Albany Times-Union, Albany Knickerbocker News, Baltimore News/American, Daily Southeast News (Downey, CA), Edwardsville (IL), Intelligencer, Hearst Community Newspapers, Inc., Los Angeles, Huntington Park (CA) Daily Signal, Huron (MI) Daily Tribune, Los Angeles Herald Examiner, Midland (MI) Daily News, Midland (TX) Reporter-Telegram, Plainview (TX) Daily Herald, San Antonio Light, San Francisco Examiner, Seattle Post-Intelligencer.

HOUSE BEAUTIFUL

1700 Broadway

(212) 903-5000

No bureaus.

THE JOURNAL OF COMMERCE

110 Wall St., N.Y. 10005

(212) 425-1616

The Journal of Commerce is not a small circulation version of The Wall Street Journal. There are similarities, of course, such as Monday-through-Friday publication, but the major difference is that the relatively small circulation (23,000) Journal of Commerce provides specialized coverage of several industries, particularly commodities, imports, insurance and transportation. Bureaus and correspondents are located all over the world, including six in the U.S.

Atlanta:

127 Peachtree St., N.E., Suite 827, Atlanta 30303

(404) 525-5525, Craig Dunlap

Chicago:

77 W. Washington St., Chicago 60602

(312) 786-9426

Houston:

Suite 229, 1520 World Trade Bldg., Houston 77002

(713) 227-8670, Stanley Mantrop

New Orleans:

1026 International Trade Mart, New Orleans 70130

(504) 529-1168, Bill Mongelluzzo

San Francisco:

Rm. 607, 110 Sutter St., San Francisco 94104

(415) 433-3238, Maureen Robb

Washington, D.C.:

Rm. 300, 1319 F St., N.W., Wash., D.C.

(202) 637-3670, Tom Connors

KING FEATURES

235 E. 45 St., N.Y. 10017

(212) 682-5600

One of the world's largest newspaper syndicates. King Features is owned by the Hearst Corporation and is headquartered in the old New York Mirror building, where a few columnists, including Phyllis Battelle and Ralph Hollenbeck, have offices.

Following are the addresses of other columnists:

Joyce Brothers, 1530 Palisade Ave., Fort Lee, N.J. 07024

Dr. Lester L. Coleman, 114 E. 72nd St., N.Y. 10021

Melvin Durslag, Los Angeles Herald-Examiner, L.A. 90054

Marianne Means, 1701 Pennsylvania Ave., N.W., Wash, D.C. 20006

Jack O'Brian, Station WOR, 1440 Broadway, N.Y. 10018

Kevin P. Phillips, 4312 Montgomery Ave., Bethesda, Md. 20014

Nicholas von Hoffman, 1632 Riggs Place, N.W., Wash., D.C. 20009

McCALL'S

230 Park Ave., N.Y. 10017

(212) 551-9500

No bureaus.

McGRAW-HILL WORLD NEWS SERVICE

1221 Ave. of the Americas, N.Y. 10020

(212) 512-2000

L.C. Peter Gall is director of this sizeable operation (38 full-time correspondents in seven domestic bureaus plus many stringers).

Atlanta:

Suite 610, 235 Peachtree St., N.E., Atlanta 30319

(404) 521-3287, Inge Kummant

Chicago:

645 North Michigan Ave., Chicago 60611

(312) 751-3700, Jeff Ryser

Dallas:

Suite 907, 5151 Beltline Rd., Dallas 75240

(214) 458-2400, Lorraine Smith

Detroit:

3756 City Natl. Bank Bldg., Detroit 48226

(313) 962-5600, David Whiteside

Houston:

        375 Dresser Tower, 601 Jefferson St., Houston 77002

        (713) 659-4558, Eric Johnson

Los Angeles:

        3200 Wilshire Blvd., L.A. 90010

        (213) 487-1160, Barbara Lamb

San Francisco:

        425 Battery St., San Francisco 94111

        (415) 362-4600, Margaret Ralston Drossel

Washington, D.C.:

        1120 Vermont Ave., N.W., Wash., D.C. 20045

        (202) 463-1600, Robert E. Farrell

The McGraw-Hill News bureaus service all of these publications:

American Machinist

Architectural Record

Aviation Week

Biotechnology Newswatch

Chemical Engineering

Chemical Week (also Chemical Week Newswire)

Coal Age/Coal Week

Data Communications

Electrical Wholesaling

Electrical Week

Electronics

Engineering and Mining Journal

Engineering News-Record

Fleet Owner

Green Markets

International Construction Week

International Management

Metals Week (also Metalsweek Insider Report)

Modern Plastics

Modern Plastics International

Nuclear Fuel

Nucleonics Week

Oilgram News

Oilgram Price Report

Physician and Sportsmedicine

SynFuels

Textile World

      Separate listings for Aviation Week, Business Week, Electrical World, and Electronics appear elsewhere.

College and University Business, National Petroleum News, Nation's Schools, Postgraduate Medicine, Power and Securities Week also are McGraw-Hill publications, but are not serviced by the McGraw-Hill News Service.

MECHANIX ILLUSTRATED
1515 Broadway, N.Y. 10036
(212) 719-6000
No bureaus.

MERCHANDISING
1515 Broadway, N.Y. 10036
(212) 869-1300
A monthly Gralla publication, Merchandising covers electronics, housewares and major appliances.

Chicago:
3525 W. Peterson Ave., Chicago 60659
(312) 463-1102, Debbie Rosenblum
Los Angeles:
16200 Ventura Blvd., Encino 91436
(213) 788-0271, Deborah Cromer

MOTOR MAGAZINE
555 W. 57 St., N.Y. 10019
(212) 262-8616
Detroit:
29226 Orchard Lake Rd., Suite 20, Farmington Hills 48018
(313) 626-3366, Robert J. Lund

MOTOR BOATING & SAILING
224 W. 57 St., N.Y. 10019
(212) 262-8768
Costa Mesa:
1638-G Placentia Ave., Costa Mesa 92627
(714) 642-5410, Val Ely
Sausalito:
3030 Bridgewood, Sausalito 94965
(415) 332-6750, Chris Volger

NEWSPAPER ENTERPRISE ASSOCIATION
200 Park Ave., N.Y. 10166
(212) 557-5870

Los Angeles:

>1665 N. Beverly Dr., Beverly Hills 90210
>
>(213) 271-0136, Dick Kleiner

NEA is one of the world's largest feature news services, with more than 700 client newspapers in North America. In 1978, the company moved to the Pan Am Building and became part of United Media Enterprises, Inc., which includes United Feature Syndicate.

NEA staff writers are interested in exclusive photos, features and article suggestions. Following are the special interests of several columnists:

>Tom Tiede—national correspondent
>
>Robert Walters—commentary—777 14 St., N.W., Wash., D.C.
>
>Bob Wagman
>
>Murray Olderman—sports—Box 6346, Incline Village, NV 89450
>
>Howard Siner—sports
>
>Aileen Claire Snoddy—food
>
>Ellie Grossman—women's news

Others (who are listed in the book, Syndicated Columnists) include Julian Bond, Don Graff, David Handler and William Rusher.

There is a close relationship between NEA and Scripps-Howard.

NEWSWEEK

>444 Madison Ave., N.Y. 10022
>
>(212) 350-2000

Circulation in 1983 was over 3 million. Newsweek does not change bureau personnel and locations as much as other news weeklies. The Washington bureau is the largest—28 reporters and photographers, headed by one of Washington's senior correspondents, Mel Elfin. Denver and Miami bureaus recently were opened.

Boston:

>185 Dartmouth St., Boston 02116
>
>(617) 262-5232, Sylvester Monroe

Denver:

>1420 Larimer St., Denver 80202
>
>(303) 592-1300, Jeff B. Copland

Atlanta:

>1120 Gaslight Tower, 235 Peachtree N.E., Atlanta 30303
>
>(404) 581-0000, Vern Smith

Boston:

>185 Dartmouth St., Boston 02116
>
>(617) 262-5232, Sylvester Monroe

Chicago:

>200 E. Randolph Dr., Chicago 60601
>
>(312) 861-1180, Frank Maier

Denver:

    1420 Larimer St., Denver 80202

    (303) 592-1300, Jeff B. Copeland

Detroit:

    100 Renaissance Center, Detroit 48243

    (313) 259-4833, Richard Manning

Houston:

    Pennzoil Place, South Tower, 711 Louisiana, Houston 77002

    (713) 227-2411, Stryker McGuire

Los Angeles:

    10100 Santa Monica Blvd., L.A. 90067

    (213) 553-3059, Janet Huck

Miami:

    300 Biscayne Blvd., Miami 33131

    (305) 358-2541, Ron Moreau

New York:

    444 Madison Ave., N.Y. 10022

    (212) 350-2000, Tony Fuller (In addition, Patricia N. Seth operates the United Nations bureau.)

San Francisco:

    505 Sansone St., San Francisco 94111

    (415) 788-2651, Vern Smith

Washington, D.C.:

    1750 Pennsylvania Ave., N.W., Wash., D.C. 20006

    (202) 626-2000, Mel Elfin

NEW YORK NEWS

    220 E. 42 St., N.Y. 10017

    (212) 949-1234

Though the New York News maintains bureaus in Albany and elsewhere, editor James G. Wieghart requests that the news releases be sent to main office. Eight editions are published for suburban, New Jersey, New York and Connecticut, and each of the five boroughs, Manhattan, Brooklyn, Bronx, Queens and Staten Island. The combined circulation makes the News the largest newspaper in the country. Circulation in 1983 was about 1.4 million daily and 1.9 million Sunday.

    A large bureau operates in Washington, D.C.:

    2101 L St., N.W., Wash., D.C. 20037

    (202) 467-6670, Lars-Erik-Nelson

The Tribune Syndicate, which is headquartered in the News building, distributes columnists of the News, including Liz Smith, Douglas Watt, Kay Gardella and Jimmy Breslin.

NEW YORK POST

210 South St., N.Y. 10002

(212) 349-5000

Since purchasing the Post (founded in 1801) in early 1977, Rupert Murdoch has made countless changes. Some critics are disturbed by the changes but the fact is that circulation has zoomed from about 500,000 to over 950,000, bureaus have been set up throughout the area (the Post previously only had bureaus in Albany and Washington) and the Post now provides more news than ever before. Two full-time reporters are maintained at City Hall and one reporter is at Police Headquarters. Local editions now are published for Long Island and Westchester. In 1980, the Post launched all-day publication.

Albany:

Pressroom, State Capitol, Albany 12224

(518) 465-9623, Fred Dicker

Bronx:

Pressroom, Bronx County Courthouse, 851 Grand Concourse Ave., Bronx 10451

(212) 590-8300, Al Sostehen

Brooklyn:

Pressroom, Federal Court House, 225 Cadman Plaza East, Brooklyn 11201

(212) 330-7278, Jerry Capeci

Mineola:

Pressroom, Supreme Court Bldg., Mineola 11501

(516) 535-2780, Bob Weddle

Queens:

175-61 Hillside Ave., Jamaica 11432

(212) 520-5895-5897, Jerry Peritz

Westchester:

County Office Bldg., 148 Martine Ave., White Plains 10601

(914) 761-0903

Washington, D.C.:

#440, 1333 H St., N.W. Wash., D.C. 20005

(202) 393-1531

THE NEW YORK TIMES

229 W. 43 St., N.Y. 10036

(212) 556-1234

Albany:

Press Rm., State Capitol, Albany 12224

(518) 436-0757, Michael Oreskes

Atlanta:

229 Peachtree St., N.E., Atlanta 30303

(404) 524-2410, William Schmidt

Boston:
>15 Court Sq., Boston 02108
>(627) 720-0727, Fox Butterfield

Chicago:
>11 E. Walton Pl., Chicago 60611
>(312) 943-2535, Andrew H. Malcolm

Denver:
>2727 Bryant St., Denver 80211
>(303) 445-5570, William Schmidt

Detroit:
>845 Free Press Bldg., Detroit 48226
>(313) 961-7858, John Holusha

Houston:
>801 Congress St., Houston 77002
>(713) 227-2638, Wayne King

Los Angeles:
>Statler Center Bldg., 900 Wilshire Blvd., L.A. 90017
>(213) 624-2349, Bob Lindsey
>(Hollywood correspondent Aljean Harmetz is at 2065 Kerwood Ave.,
>L.A. 90025.)

Miami:
>Suite 2806, 100 N. Biscayne Blvd., Miami 33132
>(305) 358-5585, Reginal Stuart

Philadelphia:
>570 Lindsey Dr., Philadelphia 19087
>(215) 964-8828, William Robbins

San Francisco:
>925 Fox Plaza Bldg., San Francisco 94102
>(415) 861-8662, Wallace Turner

Trenton:
>Press Rm., State House, W. State St., Trenton 08625
>(609) 292-2121, Joe Sullivan

Washington, D.C.:
>1000 Connecticut Ave., N.W., Wash., D.C. 20036
>(202) 862-0300, Ben Franklin

The New York Times News Service distributes the columns of James Reston, Tom Wicker, William Safire and Russell Baker of the N.Y. and Washington bureaus to quite a few major newspapers. The Times bureau in Washington, with over 65 people, is the largest in the Capital and one of the most important bureaus in the world.

The New York Times operates the largest national bureau system of any general newspaper. The Times also has large staffs of reporters who write for Sunday sections in Long Island, Westchester and Connecticut. Suburban and other editors are located in New York, and assignments are handled by the metropolitan desk. A bureau at the United Nations is operated by Richard Bernstein.

The Times also has a bureau in Room 9 of City Hall, N.Y.10007, headed by Millie Goodwin (212) 556-1947.

Daily circulation of the morning Times increased in 1983 to a 10-year high of 913,000, fourth largest in the country. Sunday circulation increased to 1,523,000, second largest in the country.

Following is a list of suburban bureaus:

Connecticut:
51 Bank St., Stamford 06901
(203) 324-9340, Susan Chira; Hartford correspondent is at
(203) 247-2991.

Long Island:
1225 Franklin Ave., Garden City 11530
(516) 747-0511

Northern New Jersey:
Press Rm., Bergen County Court Bldg., Hackensack 07601
(201) 646-3420

Westchester:
170 Hamilton Ave., White Plains 10601
(914) 949-0984, James Feron

OFFICIAL AIRLINE GUIDES, INC.

888 Seventh Ave., N.Y. 10106
(212) 977-8300

Travel Magazines Division of Official Airlines Guides, Inc. (a Dun & Bradstreet Company) publishes nine magazines.

AirCargo Magazine
Frequent Flyer
TravelScene (formerly Air Travel)
TravelAge East
TravelAge MidAmerica
TravelAge SouthEast
TravelAge West
travel management newsletter (also travel management daily)

Martin B. Deutsch is editor and publisher of the nine publications. Each has a separate staff in New York, but uses the same bureaus:

Chicago:
2416 Prudential Plaza, Chicago 60601
(312) 861-0432, Linda Smith-Jessup

Los Angeles:
1717 N. Highland Ave., L.A. 90028
(213) 466-3265, Gerald Orlin

Pacific:
1114 Wilder Ave., Honolulu 96822
(808) 524-5424, Jodi Belknap

San Francisco:
>582 Market St., San Francisco 94104
>
>(415) 781-8353, Donald Langley

Washington, D.C.:
>1625 Eye St., Wash., D.C. 20006
>
>(202) 659-4525, Barbara Cook

OUTDOOR LIFE

>380 Madison Ave., N.Y. 10017
>
>(212) 687-3000
>
>Circulation 1,500,000. A Times Mirror monthly magazine. Mail is for-

warded to the regional editors. Mike Toth (East), Frank Sargeant (South),
Gerald Bethge (Midwest), and Jim LaRocco (West).

PARADE

>750 Third Ave., N.Y. 10017
>
>(212) 573-7000

Washington, D.C.:
>1401-16 St., N.W., Wash., D.C. 20006
>
>(202) 483-4744, Jack Anderson, Mike Satchell

>1983 circulation of Parade, the Sunday supplement, was over 24

million! A major boost came in late 1983 when the N.Y. News was added.

PENTHOUSE

>1965 Broadway, N.Y. 10023
>
>(212) 496-6100

Los Angeles:
>924 Westwood Blvd., L.A. 90024
>
>(213) 824-9831

PEOPLE

>1271 Ave., of the Americas, N.Y. 10020
>
>(212) 586-1212

Boston:
>302 Berkeley St., Boston 02116
>
>(617) 247-4769, Gail Jennes

Chicago:
>303 E. Ohio St., Chicago 60611
>
>(312) 329-6800, Linda Witt

Houston:
>1913 Gardenia St., Houston 77018
>
>(713) 681-0478, Kent Demaret

Los Angeles:
>450 N. Roxbury Dr., Beverly Hills 90210
>
>(213) 273-1530

San Francisco:
>>100 Bush St., San Francisco 94104
>>(415) 982-5000, Nancy Faber
Washington, D.C.:
>>888 16 St., N.W., Wash., D.C. 20006
>>(202) 293-4300, Garry Clifford

POPULAR MECHANICS
>>224 W. 57 St., N.Y. 10019
>>(212) 262-4815
Detroit:
>>1302 W. Lafayette Tower, 1321 Orleans, Detroit 48207
>>(313) 962-0318, Daniel C. Ross
Western:
>>Box 7607, Stockton, CA 95207
>>(209) 931-1056, Mike Lamm
>>The bureaus are primarily for automotive news.

REUTERS
>>1700 Broadway, N.Y. 10019
>>(212) 582-4030
>>Reuters, the global news organization headquartered in England, has had several U.S. bureaus for many years and has become increasingly important in North America. Desmond Maberley is editor; Brian Bain is news editor; Margaret Klein is managing editor and Geoffrey Atkins is commodity news editor in the Chicago bureau.
>>The U.S. operation serves a large number of major U.S. newspapers, radio and TV stations, brokers, banks, commodity traders and other subscribers.

Chicago:
>>141 W. Jackson Blvd., Chicago 60604
>>(312) 922-6030, Felix Sergio
Dallas:
>>442 Communications Ctr., Dallas 75265
>>(214) 698-9758, David W. Finch
Detroit:
>>321 Lafayette Blvd., Detroit 48231
>>(313) 961-8371, John Stark
Houston:
>>1 Allen Center, Houston 77002
>>(713) 659-2450, Allen Van Cranebrock
Kansas City:
>>4800 Main St., Kansas City, MO 64112
>>(816) 561-8671, Dan Ruck

118

Los Angeles:
> 3407 W. 6 St., L.A. 90020
>
> (213) 380-2014, Ronald C. Clarke

Miami:
> 121 S.E. First St., Miami 33131
>
> (305) 374-5013, Stewart Russell

United Nations:
> Room C-316, United Nations, N.Y. 10017
>
> (212) 355-6053, G.M. Littlejohns

Washington, D.C.:
> 1333 H St., N.W., Wash., D.C. 20005
>
> (202) 628-9212, Bruce Russell

ROLLING STONE

> 745 Fifth Ave., N.Y. 10151
>
> (212) 758-3800

Los Angeles:
> Suite 3740, 1 Century Plaza, 2029 Century Park E., L.A. 90067
>
> (213) 553-9414

Started by Jann Wenner in San Francisco in 1967, Rolling Stone now has a biweekly circulation of 775,000. The operation is centralized in New York, with an office in Los Angeles. Releases should be sent to Mr. Wenner, who is editor and publisher, and to David Rosenthal who is managing editor.

SEVENTEEN

> 850 Third Ave., N.Y. 10022
>
> (212) 759-8100

With a monthly circulation of 1.6 million, Seventeen is the largest circulation magazine in its field (young women, 13 to 20). No bureaus.

SPORT MAGAZINE

> 119 W. 40 St., N.Y. 10018
>
> (212) 869-4700
>
> No bureaus.

SPORTS AFIELD

> 250 W. 55 St., N.Y. 10019
>
> (212) 262-8835
>
> No bureaus.

SPORTS ILLUSTRATED

> 1271 Ave. of the Americas, N.Y. 10020
>
> (212) 841-3105

Time, Fortune and Sports Illustrated have separate staffs, though all utilize the Time-Life News Service. The Sports Illustrated staff is supplemented by correspondents in more than 60 cities, from Albuquerque to Winston-Salem, Many of the local correspondents are well-known sports writers on their local newspapers. The names of other correspondents are listed in the magazine, but all correspondence should be channeled through Eleanore Milosovic, chief of correspondents.

Los Angeles:

280 S. Beverly Dr., Beverly Hills 90212

(213) 858-1591, Denise Hall

Washington, D.C.:

1333 H St., N.W., Wash., D.C. 20005

(202) 371-1787, Norma Langley

TELEVISION/RADIO AGE

1270 Ave. of the Americas, N.Y. 10020

(212) 757-8400

Washington, D.C.:

716 W. Wayne St., Arlington, VA 22204

(703) 521-4187, Howard Fields

TIME

1271 Ave. of the Americas, N.Y. 10020

(212) 586-1212

Time's 85 editions are printed in 15 cities around the world, which means that the staff at the Time-Life Building in Rockefeller Center coordinates a huge, complex operation. Richard L. Duncan is Chief of Correspondents of the Time-Life News Service. This includes hundreds of correspondents and stringers in bureaus in 21 countries.

Following are the ten domestic bureaus.:

Atlanta:

Suite 2501, 233 Peachtree St., N.E., Atlanta 30303

(404) 659-8050, Joseph Boyce

Boston:

277 Dartmouth St., Boston 02116

(617) 262-7551

Chicago:

303 E. Ohio St., Chicago 60611

(312) 329-7860, Christopher Ogden

Denver:

2060 Dexter St., Denver 80207

(303) 320-1141, Robert Wurmstedt

Detroit:
> 1510 Fisher Bldg., West Grand & Second Blvds., Detroit 77002
>
> (713) 759-0907, Robert Wurmstedt

Houston:
> 1125 Commerce Bldg., 914 Main St., Houston 77002
>
> (713) 759-0907, David Jackson

Los Angeles:
> 450 N. Roxbury Dr., Beverly Hills 90210
>
> (213) 273-1530, Benjamin Cate

New York:
> 23rd Flr., Time-Life Bldg., Rockefeller Center, N.Y. 10020
>
> (212) 841-2980, Peter Stoler

San Francisco:
> 100 Bush St., San Francisco 94104
>
> (415) 982-5000, Eileen Shields

Washington, D.C.:
> 888 16th St., N.W., Wash., D.C. 20006
>
> (202) 293-4300, Robert Ajemian

TRAVELAGE EAST
TRAVELAGE SOUTHEAST
TRAVEL MANAGEMENT DAILY
TRAVEL MANAGEMENT NEWSLETTER
> 888 Seventh Ave., N.Y. 10106
>
> (212) 977-8300

Atlanta:
> 40 Peachtree Valley Rd., N.E., Atlanta 30309
>
> (404) 351-8262, Nancy Lesure

Chicago:
> 2416 Prudential Plaza, Chicago 60601
>
> (312) 861-0432, Linda Smith-Jessup

Honolulu:
> 1860 Ala Moana Blvd., Honolulu 96815
>
> (808) 955-7486, Jeri Bostwic

Los Angeles:
> 2999 Overland Ave., L.A. 90064
>
> (213) 204-1184, Gerald Orlin, Lorraine June

Miami:
> 555 N. Birds St., Fort Lauderdale 33304
>
> (305) 945-8778, Marilyn Springer

San Francisco:
> 582 Market St., San Francisco 94104
>
> (415) 781-8353, Donald C. Langley

121

Washington, D.C.:

    1625 Eye St., N.W., Wash., D.C. 20006

    (202) 659-4525, Barbara Cook

    Travelage publications are published by Official Airlines Guides, Inc., a Dun & Bradstreet Company. Also published at this office (one floor above the publisher of News Bureaus) is Frequent Flyer.

TRAVEL & LEISURE

    1120 Ave. of the Americas, N.Y. 10036

    (212) 399-2500

    Monthly circulation 960,000. Owned by American Express. No bureaus.

TRAVEL TRADE

    6 E. 46 St., N.Y. 10017

    (212) 883-1110

Florida:

    1 Lincoln Rd., Miami Beach 33139

    (305) 531-8116, Ethel Blum

Illinois:

    948 Waukegan Rd., Deerfield 60015

    (312) 222-3955, John A. Handley

Washington, D.C.:

    3611 39 St., N.W., Wash., D.C. 20016

    (202) 363-7316, Don Knoles

TRAVEL WEEKLY

    One Park Ave., N.Y. 10016

    (212) 725-3600

Chicago:

    R.D. 4, Monmouth 61462

    (312) 734-5014, Robert Grimsley

Honolulu:

    708 Koko Isle Circle, Honolulu 96825

    (808) 395-8703, Tony Bartlett

Los Angeles:

    3460 Wilshire Blvd., Beverly Hills 90010

    (213) 387-2100, Jerry Brown

Miami:

    444 Brickell Ave., Miami 33131

    (305) 374-1300, Ernest Blum

San Francisco:

    2203 Jones St., San Francisco 94133

    (415) 885-6618, Janet Felix

Washington, D.C.:

> 1156 15 St., N.W., Wash., D.C. 20005
> (202) 293-3400, Fran Durbin

UNITED FEATURE SYNDICATE

> 200 Park Ave., N.Y. 10155
> (212) 557-2333

This company moved in 1978 from the N.Y. Daily News Bldg. to the Pan Am Bldg. and merged with the Newspaper Enterprise Association (NEA) to form United Media Enterprises, Inc. NEA is listed separately.

In 1980, Independent News Alliance was formed to replace North American News Alliance (NANA) and Women's News Service.

Following are the addresses of several UFS columnists:

Jack Anderson, 1401 16 St., N.W., Wash., D.C. 20036

Donald Lambro, 6605 Greenview Lane, Springfield, VA 22152

Robert S. Wagman, 8806 First Ave., Silver Spring, Md. 20910

Others listed in the book, Syndicated Columnists, include Joan Crosby, Dr. Michael Fox, John Hess, Charles Hix, John Lofton, Emily Malino, Virginia Payette, Florence de Santis and Jack Smith

INA and Scripps-Howard News Service have a Washington bureau at 1110 Vermont Ave., N.W., Wash., D.C. 20005, (202) 833-9520.

UNITED PRESS INTERNATIONAL

> 1400 I St., Wash., D.C. 20005
> (202) 289-0909

In 1984, UPI moved its world headquarters to Washington, D.C., though several departments (including financial) remain in New York at

> 220 E. 42 St., N.Y. 10017
> (212) 850-8600

UPI opened over 30 new bureaus in 1982 and 1983 and now has over 250 news and picture bureaus serving about 1,600 daily newspapers and 4,000 stations throughout the world. In the U.S., UPI reorganized its 9 regions into these six divisions:

> *Northeast Division:* 20 Ashburton Pl., Boston 02108
> *Eastern Division:* 7 Wood St., Pittsburgh 15222
> *Southern Division:* 1819 Peachtree Rd., Atlanta 30367
> *Southwest Division:* 13900 Midway Rd., Dallas 75234
> *Central Division:* 360 N. Michigan Ave., Chicago 60611
> *Pacific Division:* Box 4329, 9th & Market St., San Francisco 94102

A UPI office is located in many major cities, as follows:

Alabama:

> 2200 Fourth Ave., N., Birmingham 35203
> (205) 328-4242

Box 1306, Montgomery 36102
(205) 262-1951

Arizona:

Box 4066, Commerce Sta., Phoenix 85030
(602) 252-5641
Box 2868, Tucson 87502
(602) 623-6409

Arkansas:

302 Gazette Bldg., Little Rock 72201
(501) 375-5559

California:

Fresno Bee Bldg., 1626 E St., Fresno 93786
(209) 237-7469
316 West 2nd Street, Los Angeles 90012
(213) 620-1230
925 L St., Ste 1185, Sacramento 95814
(916) 445-7755
Box 191, San Diego 92112
(714) 291-1815
1212 Fox Plaza, Ninth & Market Sts., San Francisco 94102
(415) 552-5900
700 W. Hedding, San Jose 95110
(408) 294-4611

Colorado:

720 South Colorado Blvd., Denver 80222
(303) 758-2002

Connecticut:

770 Asylum Ave., Hartford 06105
(203) 249-5659
40 Sargent Dr., New Haven 06511
(203) 776-4883

Delaware:

1216 King Street, Wilmington 19801
(302) 654-4330

District of Columbia:

1400 I St., N.W., Washington 20005
(202) 289-0909

Florida:

1000 Riverside Avenue, Ste. 308, Jacksonville 32204
(904) 356-2877
260 NE 17th Terrace, Miami 33132
(305) 373-7685
Box 3069, Orlando 32802
(305) 422-8051

Box 1704, Pensacola 32522
(904) 455-2688
Box 164, Tallahassee 32302
(904) 222-1317
Box 191, Tampa 33601
(813) 228-8752

Georgia:

1819 Peachtree Rd., N.E., Atlanta 30367
(404) 355-3700
1001 Abercorn St., Savannah 31406
(912) 927-7627

Hawaii:

Box 3110, Honolulu 96802
(808) 533-1828

Idaho:

Box 413, Boise 83701
(208) 342-6621

Illinois:

509 S. Neil St., Champaign 61820
(217) 356-6095
360 N. Michigan Ave., Chicago 60611
(312) 781-1600
Republican Bldg. Marion 62959
(618) 993-5796
Press Room, State Capitol, Springfield 62706
(217) 525-2326

Indiana:

Box 7043, Indianapolis 46207
(317) 634-6592
WSBT Bldg., 300 W. Jefferson Blvd., South Bend 46601
(219) 289-5802

Iowa:

111 E. 3rd Street, Davenport, 52801
(319) 324-2351
Bank Bldg., 6th & Locust, Des Moines 50309
(515) 244-5185

Kansas:

Press Room, 135 N. Statehouse, Topeka 66612
(913) 233-8555
209 E. William, Ste. 210, Wichita 67202
(316) 267-9940

Kentucky:

State Capitol Bldg., Press Road, Frankfort 40601
(502) 223-8632

222 S. First St., Louisville 40202

(502) 587-5790

Louisiana:

Box 44132, Baton Rouge 70804

(504) 344-0870

1440 Canal St., Ste. 811, New Orleans 70112

(504) 581-6371

504 Texas St., Shreveport 71101

(318) 424-6420

Maine:

Box 790, Augusta 04330

(207) 623-9275

Press Herald Bldg., 390 Congress St., Portland 04111

(207) 775-7705

Maryland:

Box 347, Annapolis 21404

(301) 269-5518

News American Bldg., Lombard & South Sts., Baltimore 21203

(301) 539-6446

Massachusetts:

20 Ashburton Pl., Boston 02108

(617) 227-4000

10 Chestnut St., Springfield 01103

(413) 736-4646

Michigan:

945 Free Press Bldg., 321 W. Lafayette, Detroit 48226

(313) 965-7950

Box 2162, Grand Rapids 49501

(616) 459-5519

Box 15055, Lansing 48904

(517) 482-1923

Minnesota:

301 4th Ave., S., Minneapolis 55415

(612) 338-7547

200 State Capitol, St. Paul 55101

(612) 224-8160

Mississippi:

Box 1124, Jackson 39205

(601) 353-2907

Missouri:

Box 1, Jefferson City 65102

(314) 634-4660

4720 Oak St., Kansas City 64112

(816) 756-1881

900 N. 12th St., St. Louis 63101
(314) 231-6644

Montana:

2021 11th Ave., Helena 59604
(406) 442-6470

Nebraska:

Box 80696, Journal Bldg., Lincoln 68501
(402) 476-0381
Box 1336, Omaha 68101
(402) 346-6868

Nevada:

State Supreme Court Bldg., Carson City 89701
(702) 885-5032
Box 1088, Las Vegas 89101
(702) 384-4915
955 Kuenzli St., Reno 89520
(702) 322-1142

New Hampshire:

Box 1475, Concord 03301
(603) 224-2351

New Jersey:

1914 Atlantic Ave., Atlantic City 08401
(609) 344-8323
Box 10140, Federal Square, Newark 07101
(201) 643-1887
500 Perry St., Trenton Times Bldg., Trenton 06805
(609) 392-0700

New Mexico:

Drawer U., Albuquerque 87103
(505) 247-4196
Box 1798, Santa Fe 87501
(505) 983-3112

New York:

645 Albany Shaker Rd., Albany 12221
(518) 458-7833
1 News Plaza, Buffalo 14240
(716) 852-2085
220 East 42 St., N.Y. 10017
(212) 850-8600
131 State Supreme Courthouse, 100 Supreme Court Dr.,
Mineola 11501
(516) 477-8050
WHAM, 350 East Ave., Rochester 14604
(716) 454-4444

Box 4915, Clinton Square, Syracuse 13221
(315) 472-6391
Room 224, 148 Martine Ave., White Plains 10805
(914) 428-6178

North Carolina:

Box 32878, Charlotte 28232
(704) 334-4691
Box 2200, Raleigh 27602
(919) 833-3685

Ohio:

800 Broadway, Cincinnati 45202
(513) 721-0345
401 Euclid Avenue, Cleveland 44114
(216) 771-3455
50 W. Broad St., Columbus 43215
(614) 221-4291
125 South Superior St., Toledo 43602
(419) 242-4063
101 W. Boardsman St., Youngstown 44501
(216) 744-5802

Oklahoma:

3601 N. Lincoln Blvd., Oklahoma City 73105
(405) 843-8814
324 Main Mall, Suite 913, Tulsa 74103
(918) 587-3788

Oregon:

Fir at Sixth St., Medford 97501
(503) 776-4382
Oregonian Bldg., 1320 S.W. Broadway, Portland 97201
(503) 226-2644
Room 40, Capitol Bldg., Salem 97310
(503) 363-1918

Pennsylvania:

810 Payne-Shoemaker Bldg., 240 N. Third St., Harrisburg 17101
(717) 234-4189
1819 JFK Blvd., Suite 400, Philadelphia 19103
(215) 563-6008
Conestoga Bldg., 7 Wood St., Pittsburgh 15222
(412) 553-5300
338 N. Washington, Scranton 18501
(717) 346-6908

Rhode Island:

State House, Rm. 10, Providence 02903
(401) 351-5955

South Dakota:
>   Box 459, Pierre 57501
>   (605) 224-8843
>   112 East 13th St., Sioux Falls 57102
>   (605) 334-4825

Tennessee:
>   400 East 11th St., Chattanooga 37401
>   (615) 265-4823
>   701 Lynn Garden Dr., Kingsport 37662
>   (615) 246-8366
>   News-Sentinel Bldg., Knoxville 37902
>   (615) 525-3162
>   Commercial Appeal & Press-Scimitar Bldg., Memphis 38101
>   (901) 525-0611
>   Box 942, Nashville 37202
>   (615) 242-7348

Texas:
>   Box 12187, Capitol Sta., Austin 78711
>   (512) 472-2471
>   13900 Midway Rd., Dallas 75234
>   (214) 980-8331
>   The El Paso Herald Post, Kansas-At-Mills, Box 20, El Paso
>   (915) 542-0546
>   708 Main St., Rm. 825, Houston 77002
>   (713) 227-2171
>   Box 491, Lubbock 79408
>   (806) 765-8289
>   Box 2161, San Antonio 78297
>   (512) 222-1816

Utah:
>   Box 1375, Salt Lake City 84110
>   (801) 328-8866

Vermont:
>   Box 611, Montpelier 05602
>   (802) 223-7201

Virginia:
>   Room 255, 150 West Brambleton Ave., Norfolk 23501
>   (804) 625-5964
>   Box 1578, Richmond 23213
>   (804) 644-0701
>   145 West Campbell, Roanoke 24011
>   (703) 985-0540

Washington:
> Box 1697, Olympia 98507
> (206) 753-6534
> Post-Intelligencer Bldg., 6th & Wall Sts., Seattle 98111
> (206) 622-2505
> Box 37, Spokane 99210
> (509) 328-9483

West Virginia:
> Box 2946, Charleston 25330
> (304) 343-7560
> 343 High St., Morgantown 26505
> (304) 292-6758

Wisconsin:
> Box 1408, Madison 53701
> (608) 255-6779
> 918 N. 4 St., Rm. 214, Milwaukee 53203
> (414) 271-6588

Wyoming:
> Box 1383, Cheyenne 82001
> (307) 634-2850

UNITED STATES TOBACCO AND CANDY JOURNAL

> 254 W. 31 St., N.Y. 10001
> (212) 594-4120
> No bureaus. The same company also publishes Convenience Store
News, Electronic Industry, Smokeshop and Gaming Business.

US

> 215 Lexington Ave., N.Y. 10016
> (212) 340-7500

Los Angeles:
> 9441 Wilshire Blvd., Beverly Hills 90212
> (213) 273-1081, Rana Arons

VARIETY

> 154 W. 46 St., N.Y. 10036
> (212) 869-5700

Chicago:
> 400 N. Michigan Ave., Chic. 60611
> (312) 337-4984, Morry Roth

Los Angeles:
> 1400 N. Cahuenga Blvd., Hollywood 90028
> (213) 469-1141, Thomas M. Pryor

Washington, D.C.:

    1483 Chain Bridge Rd., McLean, VA

    (703) 448-0510, Paul Harris

    Variety, the weekly bible of show business, also owns and operates Daily Variety at the same location as its Hollywood bureau. Variety also receives reports, items and reviews from stringers in every state.

VOGUE

    350 Madison Ave., N.Y. 10017

    (212) 880-8800

    This influential monthly Conde Nast magazine (circulation 950,000) does not maintain bureaus, though it has several editors outside of N.Y.C.

THE WALL STREET JOURNAL

    22 Cortlandt St., N.Y. 10007

    (212) 285-5000

    Among the many tributes to the success of The Wall Street Journal, here are several indications of its stability and scope. Since the publication in 1972 of the first edition of this directory, the WSJ has not closed any bureaus, has added six bureaus and has increased in circulation to over 2,000,000.* Four editions are published (at 17 printing plants!) of this extraordinary five-days-a-week newspaper—Eastern, Midwest, Southwest and Western—but editorial content is the same in each edition. Publicists should send releases to the bureau nearest to the headquarters of the company, according to Managing Editor Norman Pearlstine.

Atlanta:

    6 Piedmont Center N.E., Atlanta 30305

    (404 233-2831, Eric Morgenthaler

Boston:

    35 Congress St., Boston 02109

    (617) 742-5600, June Kronholz

Chicago:

    200 W. Monroe St., Chicago 60603

    (312) 648-7600, A. Richard Martin

Cleveland:

    1325 Lakeside Ave., Cleveland 44114

    (216) 241-5183, Paul Ingrasia

Dallas:

    1233 Regal Row, Dallas 75247

    (313) 963-7800, Douge Sease

Houston:

    2770 Texas Commerce Towers, 601 Travis St., Houston 77002

    (713) 227-5440, George Getschow

Los Angeles:
>514 Shatto Pl., L.A. 90020

>(213) 383-9090, Barney Calame

Minneapolis:
>648 Baker Bldg., Minneapolis 55402

>(612) 375-0680, Claudia Waterloo

Philadelphia:
>12 S. Broad St., Phil. 19107

>(215) 893-4900, Frank Allen

Pittsburgh:
>1 Oliver Pl., Pittsburgh 15222

>(412) 471-1904, Dan Austin

St. Louis:
>769 Equitable Bldg., 10 Broadway, St. Louis 53102

>(314) 621-6566, John Curley

San Francisco:
>220 Battery St., San Francisco 94119

>(415) 986-6886, Ken Slocum

Washington, D.C.:
>1025 Connecticut Ave., Wash., D.C. 20036

>(202) 862-9200, Al Hunt

The Wall Street Journal bureaus service the Dow Jones News Service, whose subscribers include major newspapers, as well as several thousand stock brokerage firms and others with financial interests.

Dow Jones also publishes Barron's at the same address.

NEW YORK CITY BUREAUS (area code 212)

Advertising Age, 220 East 42 St., N.Y. 10017, John J. O'Connor, 210-0100

Amusement Business, 1515 Broadway, N.Y. 10036, Ancil Davis,
764-7300

Apparel News Group, 110 W. 40 St., N.Y. 10018, David Moin,
221-8288

Automotive News, 220 E. 42 St., N.Y. 10017, John Russell,
210-0100

Better Homes & Gardens, 750 Third Ave., N.Y. 10017, Margaret Baly, George Bush, 557-6600

Bon Appetit, 9 W. 57 St., N.Y. 10019, Ms. Zack Hanle, 753-6683

Broadcasting, 630 Third Ave., N.Y. 10019, Kathy Haley, 599-2830

Business Insurance, 220 E. 42 St., N.Y. 10017, Bill Densmore, 210-0139

Business Marketing, 220 E. 42 St., N.Y. 10017, Bob Donath,
210-0100

Cahners Publishing Company, 205 E. 42 St., N.Y. 10017, 949-4400

Chemical & Engineering News, 405 Lexington Ave., N.Y. 10017, William Storck, 697-3223

Chicago Tribune, Suite 2708, 220 E. 42 St., N.Y. 10017, Michael Goakley, Ken Clark, 986-0970

Christian Science Monitor, 220 E. 42 St., N.Y. 10017, John Yemma, 599-1850

Computerworld, 401 E. 80 St., N.Y. 10021, David Myers, 570-2135

Dallas Morning News, 485 Lexington Ave., N.Y. 10017, Mike Geczi, 697-8145

Dallas Times Herald, Suite 1532, 26 Broadway, N.Y. 10004, Janet Novack, 422-7781

East/West Network, 34 E. 51 St., N.Y. 10022, 888-5900

Essence, 1500 Broadway, N.Y. 10036, 730-4260

Field Newspaper Syndicate, 30 E. 42 St., N.Y. 10017, 682-5560

Gannett Co., 535 Madison Ave., N.Y. 10022, Joel Dreyfus, 715-5417

Hollywood Reporter, 1501 Broadway, N.Y. 10036, Mitchell Hall, Sharon Dobutar, 354-1858

Industry Week, 122 E. 42 St., N.Y. 10168, Marilyn Much, 867-9191

Iron Age, 825 Seventh Ave., N.Y. 10019, Bob Reyon, 245-7555

Jet, 1270 Ave. of the Americas, N.Y. 10020, 586-2911

Los Angeles Times, 220 E. 42 St., N.Y. 10017, John Goldman, 661-7110

Medical World News, 211 E. 43 St., N.Y. 10017, Malcolm Manber, Rochelle Green, 490-7817

Multichannel News, 633 Third Ave., N.Y. 10017, Joe Butle, 741-6208

Newsday, 1500 Broadway, N.Y. 10036, Dennis Duggan, 730-4350

Philadelphia Inquirer, 180 Riverside Dr., N.Y. 10024, Barbara Kantrowitz, 787-3125

Playboy, 747 Third Ave., N.Y. 10017, G. Barry Golson, 688-3030

Runner's World, 6 E. 39 St., N.Y. 10016, Stan Singer, 889-9120

Satellite Communications, 301 W. 53 St., N.Y. 10019, Jill Marks 246-7082

TV Guide, 1290 Ave. of the Americas, N.Y. 10019, Neil Hickey, 484-9900

Teen, 437 Madison Ave., N.Y. 10022, Hollie Alper, 935-9150

Television Digest, 475 Fifth Ave., N.Y. 10017, Dave Tachenbruch, 686-5410

US News & World Report, 45 Rockefeller Plaza, N.Y. 10020, Ron Scherer, 246-3366

USA Today, 535 Madison Ave., N.Y. 10022, Joel Dreyfus, 715-5410

United Press International, 220 E. 42 St., N.Y. 10017, 850-8600

Washington Post, 444 Madison Ave., N.Y. 10022, Margaret Hornblower, 350-2588

NEWSDAY

Melville, Long Island 11747

(516) 454-2020

With a 1983 circulation of over 525,000, Newsday blankets Long Island—Nassau and Suffolk counties. A "City Edition" is circulated in Queens and Manhattan. Daily circulation is 12th largest in the country and Sunday circulation of over 600,000 is the 14th largest. Mostly home-delivered, it is an evening newspaper with early deadlines, which for some departments are akin to a morning newspaper.

Albany:

Box 7255, Albany 12224

(518) 465-2311

New York:

1500 Broadway, N.Y. 10036

(212) 730-4350, Dennis Duggan

(This bureau handles national, business news and news beats.

The Long Island business editor is based in Melville.)

Riverhead:

209 W. Main St., Riverhead 11901

(516) 727-7333

Queens:

95-25 Queens Blvd., Rego Park 11374

(212) 520-0505

Washington, D.C.:

1301 Pennsylvania Ave., Wash., D.C. 20006

(202) 393-5630

THE READER'S DIGEST

Pleasantville 10570

(914) 769-7000

The Digest maintains advertising and business offices in more than 50 cities throughout the world. Editorial bureaus are located in Pleasantville, New York City (200 Park Ave.), and Washington, D.C., (1730 Rhode Island Ave.). Roving editors (full and part-time) and dozens of senior and associate editors cover the country in their quest for original articles. Article suggestions and other material should be sent to the Editors in Pleasantville. Circulation of the U.S. and international editions is about 30 million! William Schulz is bureau chief.

ROCHESTER DEMOCRAT & CHRONICLE
ROCHESTER TIMES-UNION

55 Exchange St., Rochester 14614

(716) 232-7100

Washington, D.C.:

      1627 K St., N.W., Wash., D.C. 20006

      (202) 862-4500, James Geehan

      Rochester, the state's third largest city (population 241,000) is the headquarters of the Gannett Co., the nation's largest newspaper group. The flagship newspapers are the morning Democrat and Chronicle (130,000 daily and 245,000 Sunday) and evening Times-Union (113,000). Circulation of the morning newspaper is increased in 1983 and the evening circulation declined.

GANNETT CO., INC.

      Lincoln Tower, Rochester 14614

      ~~(716) 546-8600~~ 703-284-6671

      Gannett provides considerably more information about its operations than many other publishers for several reasons, notably that it is publicly owned (New York Stock Exchange) and is the nation's largest group, or chain, of daily newspapers—86 newspapers in 37 states, with a total circulation of 3.6 million.

      In 1982, Gannett launched USA Today, the nationwide Monday-Friday newspaper that now has a circulation of over one million! Several newspapers were acquired in 1982 and 1983 and a few were merged or sold, notably the Oakland Tribune in California. The following is a list, as of 1983:

Arizona:

      Tucson/Tucson Citizen

California:

      Marin County/Independent Journal

      Salinas/Salinas Californian

      San Bernardino/The Sun

      Stockton/Stockton Record

      Visalia/Visalia Times-Delta

Colorado:

      Fort Collins/The Coloradoan

Connecticut:

      Norwich/Norwich Bulletin

Delaware:

      Wilmington/The Morning News

      Evening Journal

District of Columbia:

      USA Today (Arlington, VA)

Florida:

      Cocoa/Today

      Fort Myers/Fort Myers News-Press

      Pensacola/The Pensacola Journal

        The Pensacola News

Georgia:
>   Gainesville/The Times

Guam:
>   Agana/Pacific Daily News

Hawaii:
>   Honolulu/Honolulu Star-Bulletin

Idaho:
>   Boise/The Idaho Statesman

Illinois:
>   Danville/The Commercial-News
>   Rockford/Rockford Register-Star

Indiana:
>   Lafayette/Journal and Courier
>   Marion/Chronicle-Tribune
>   Richmond/Palladium-Item

Iowa:
>   Iowa City/Iowa City Press-Citizen

Kansas:
>   Coffeyville/The Coffeyville Journal

Louisiana:
>   Monroe/News-Star-World
>   Shreveport/The Times

Michigan:
>   Battle Creek/The Battle Creek Enquirer
>   Lansing/Lansing State Journal
>   Port Huron/Times Herald
>   Sturgis/Sturgis Journal

Minnesota:
>   St. Cloud/St. Cloud Daily Times

Mississippi:
>   Hattiesburg/The American
>   Jackson/The Clarion-Ledger
>   Jackson Daily News

Missouri:
>   Springfield/The Springfield Daily News
>   The Springfield Leader & Press

Nebraska:
>   Fremont/Fremont Tribune

Nevada:
>   Reno/Nevada State Journal
>   Reno Evening Gazette

New Jersey:
>   Bridgewater/The Courier-News
>   Camden/Courier-Post

New Mexico:
> Santa Fe/The New Mexican

New York:
> Binghamton/The Sun-Bulletin
>> The Evening Press
>
> Elmira/Star Gazette
> Ithaca/The Ithaca Journal
> New York City/El Diario-La Prensa
> Niagara Falls/Niagara Gazette
> Poughkeepsie/Poughkeepsie Journal
> Rochester/Democrat and Chronicle
>> Times-Union
>
> Saratoga Springs/The Saratogian
> Utica/The Daily Press
>> The Observer-Dispatch
>
> Westchester Rockland Newspapers
> Mamaroneck/The Daily Times
> Mount Vernon/The Daily Argus
> New Rochelle/The Standard-Star
> Nyack-Rockland/The Journal-News
> Ossining/The Citizen Register
> Port Chester/The Daily Item
> Tarrytown/The Daily News
> White Plains/The Reporter Dispatch
> Yonkers/The Herald Statesman

Ohio:
> Chillicothe/Chillicothe Gazette
> Cincinnati/The Cincinnati Enquirer
> Fremont/The News-Messenger
> Marietta/The Marietta Times
> Port Clinton/News Herald

Oklahoma:
> Muskogee/Muskogee Daily Phoenix
>> and Times-Democrat

Oregon:
> Salem/Statesman-Journal

Pennsylvania:
> Chambersburg/Public Opinion
> Lansdale/The Reporter
> New Kensington-Tarentum/Valley News Dispatch

South Dakota:
> Sioux Falls/Argus Leader

Tennessee:
> Knoxville/The Knoxville Journal
> Nashville/The Tennessean

Texas:
> El Paso/The El Paso Times

Vermont:
> Burlington/The Burlington Free Press

Virgin Islands:
> St. Thomas/Daily News

Washington:
> Bellingham/The Bellingham Herald
>
> Olympia/The Olympian

West Virginia:
> Huntington/The Herald-Dispatch

Wisconsin:
> Green Bay/Green Bay Press-Gazette
>
> Wausau/Wausau Daily Herald

Gannett weeklies include the Suburban Newspaper Group in Cherry Hill, NJ, and newspapers in Fairfield, CN.; Melbourne and Titusville, FL; Taos, NM; Bronxville and Saratoga Springs, N.Y., and New Kensington, PA.

Gannett non-dailies include newspapers in California, Connecticut, Florida, Georgia, Mississippi, New Jersey, New York and Pennsylvania, and a newspaper supplement for children, Pennywhistle Press.

Gannett News Service provides 24-hour supplementary service to Gannett media, including the company's radio and TV stations. The headquarters moved in 1982 from Washington, D.C. to the USA Today building in Arlington, Virginia, where the general manager is James Geehan. The N.Y.C. bureau also was expanded and moved to 535 Madison Avenue. Incidentally, the company name is pronounced Guh-net. Following are the bureaus:

California:
> Suite 110, 925 L Street, Sacramento 95814, Eric Brazil,
> (916) 445-5310

Florida:
> Florida Press Center, Rm. 301, 306 South Duval St., Tallahassee
> 32301, Sharen Johnson, (904) 222-8384

Illinois:
> State Capitol Bldg., Press Room - Mezzanine, Springfield 62706,
> James George, (217) 782-6292

Indiana:
> Suite 400, 150 W. Market St., Indianapolis 46204, Gene Policinski,
> (317) 634-9751

Louisiana:
> Box 44337, Capital Station, Baton Rouge 70804, John Hill,
> (504) 387-6506, (504) 342-7333

Michigan:
> 120 East Lenawee Street, Lansing 48919, Jerry Moskal,
> (517) 487-4696

New Jersey:
>
> Room 118, State House, Trenton 08625, Janet Thornpson,
> (609) 292-5052

New York:
>
> Box 7225, State Capital, Albany 12224, John Omicinski,
> (518) 436-9781
> 535 Madison Ave., New York 10022,
> (212) 715-5417, Joel Dreyfus

Ohio:
>
> Suite 700, 16 E. Broad Street, Columbus 43215, Steve Wilson,
> (614) 224-4640

Pennsylvania:
>
> Press Room, State Capital, Harrisburg 17105, Chet Czarniak,
> (717) 634-9751

Washington:
>
> 108 Insurance Bldg., Olympia State Gov't., Campus, Mail Stop AQ-01,
> Olympia 98504, Fred Olson, (206) 943-7962, (206) 753-1688

Washington, D.C.:
>
> 1000 Wilson Blvd., Arlington, VA 22209
> (703) 276-5800, Robert Dubill

SCHENECTADY GAZETTE

> 334 State St., Schenectady 12301
> (518) 374-4141

> The morning Gazette (circulation 70,000) intensively covers its area
with 10 bureaus. Area codes of all bureaus are (518).

Albany:
>
> North Rm., Wellington Hotel, State St., Albany 12055
> 434-2912, Steve Nelson, Carlo Wolff, Jon Sorenson

Albany Capitol:
>
> LCA Rm., Capitol Bldg., State St., Albany 12055
> 462-2499, Bob Groneman

Amsterdam:
>
> 38 E. Main St., Amsterdam 12010
> 843-2830, Sam Zurlo, Judy Patrick

Ballston Spa:
>
> 100 Milton Ave., Ballston Spa 12020
> 885-6705, Beanie Fraser, Steve Williams

Cobleskill:
>
> 3 Campus Court, Cobleskill 12043
> 234-7788, Les Hendrix

Colonie:
>105 Wolf Rd., Albany 12055
>458-7056, Pam Snook, Steve Goldstein

Gloversville:
>11 Church St., Gloversville 12078
>725-8412, Jim McGuire, Jon Burlingame

Jonesville:
>Main St., Clifton Park 12065
>877-8329, Lorraine Ryan

Mechanicville:
>124 4th Ave., Mechanicville 12118
>664-9707, Hal Sheehan

Saratoga Springs:
>376 Broadway, Saratoga Springs 12866
>587-1780, Jeff Wise, Lee Coleman

THE STAR
>660 White Plains Rd., Tarrytown 10591
>(914) 332-5000

Formerly called The National Star, this weekly tabloid has a circulation of over 3.5 million. It's a division of News Group Publications, which is headed by Rupert Murdoch. The editorial offices were moved in late 1983 from Manhattan to Tarrytown.

NORTH CAROLINA

THE CHARLOTTE NEWS
>Box 30308, Charlotte 28230
>(704) 379-6300

Monroe:
>304 Stevens St., Monroe 28110
>(704) 289-3928

The News also has a Raleigh bureau, but assignments are channeled via Dennis Sodomka, managing editor.

THE CHARLOTTE OBSERVER
>Box 32188, Charlotte 28232
>(704) 379-6300

The morning Observer has the state's largest circulation (170,000). Bureaus are in North and South Carolina. The evening News (circulation 52,000) is at the same headquarters building but has a separate staff. Bureaus recently were opened in Concord and Monroe in North Carolina and Lancaster in South Carolina.
North Carolina

Catawba Valley:
> 261 Second Ave., Hickory 28601
> (704) 324-0055, Bruce Henderson

Concord:
> 82 Union St., Concord 28025
> (704) 788-4178

Gastonia:
> 215 S. Broad St., Gastonia 28052
> (704) 864-4310, Wayne Nicholas, Dave Baity

Monroe:
> 138 Main St., Monroe 28110
> (704) 289-6576, Bob Glendy

Raleigh:
> Box 549, Raleigh 27602
> (919) 834-8471, Katherine White, Ken Allen

South Carolina

Columbia:
> 1138 Main St., Columbia 29201
> (803) 779-5037, Henry Eichel, Jim Walser

Rock Hill:
> Box 2913 CRS, Rock Hill 29730
> (803) 328-6915, David Perlmutt

Washington, D.C.:
> 1319 F St., N.W., Wash., D.C. 20004
> (Knight-Ridder Newspapers)
> (202) 637-3600, Bill Arthur

GREENSBORO DAILY NEWS
> Box 20848, Greensboro 27420
> (919) 373-7000

Alamance:
> Box 388, Burlington 27215
> (919) 227-6380

High Point:
> 715 N. Main St., High Point 27261
> (919) 883-4422

Raleigh:
> Box 1591, Raleigh 27602
> (919) 832-5549, Chuck Alston

Randolph:
> 2010 S. Fayetteville St., Asheboro 27203
> (919) 625-8451, Paul Kostyu

Rockingham:
> Eden Bldg., 698 Linden Dr., Eden 27288
> (919) 627-4881

THE NEWS AND OBSERVER
215 S. McDowell St., Raleigh 27602

(919) 832-1234

The morning News and Observer serve Eastern North Carolina, including the Research Triangle. Daily circulation is 130,000; Sunday circulation is 163,000. The same company publishes the afternoon Raleigh Times, which has a circulation (35,000) primarily in the capital area.

Eastern:
202 Dellwood Drive, Greenville 27834

(919) 756-3159, Jerry Allegood

Washington, D.C.:
1319 F St., N.W., Wash., D.C. 20004

(202) 637-3628, Steve Kelly

WINSTON-SALEM JOURNAL
415 N. Marshall St., Winston-Salem 27102

(919) 727-7211

Davidson county:
400 E. Center St., Lexington 27292

(704) 246-2074

Northwest:
Box 1087, N. Wilkesboro 28659

(919) 667-5691, Charlene Havnaer

Raleigh:
204 N. Person St., Raleigh 27603

(919) 833-9056, Michael Skube

Surry county:
Box 510, Mount Airy 27030

(919) 789-9338, Kenneth Haynes

Washington, D.C.:
214 Ntl. Press Bldg., Wash., D.C. 20045

(202) 347-7770, Gene Marlowe (Media General News Service)

NORTH DAKOTA

FARGO FORUM
Box 2020, 101 N. 5 St., Fargo 58102

(701) 235-7311

Largest circulation in the state—58,000 daily and 62,000 Sunday.

North Dakota:
Capitol Bldg., Bismarck 58501

(701) 224-0830, Jim Neumann

Minnesota:

> Box 69, Moorhead Center Mall, Moorhead 56560
>
> (218) 241-5553, John Sundvor

GRAND FORKS HERALD

> 114 N. 4 St., Grand Forks 58201
>
> (701) 775-4211

Bismarck:

> State Capitol Bldg., Bismarck 58505
>
> (701) 258-5633, Tim Fought

Washington, D.C.:

> 1319 F St., N.W., Washington, D.C. 20004
>
> (202) 637-3600, Jim McGregor (Knight-Ridder)

OHIO

AKRON BEACON JOURNAL

> 44 E. Exchange St., Akron 44328
>
> (216) 375-8111

Columbus:

> 16 E. Broad St., Columbus 43215
>
> (614) 224-1613, William Hershey

Washington, D.C.:

> 1319 F St., N.W., Wash., D.C. 20004
>
> (202) 637-3600, David Hess (Knight-Ridder)

THE CINCINNATI ENQUIRER

> 617 Vine St., Cincinnati 45201
>
> (513) 721-2700
>
> Established in 1841 (before the Cleveland Press and Cleveland Plain

Dealer and 40 years before the Cincinnati Post), the morning Enquirer has a
daily circulation of 192,000 and a Sunday circulation of 299,000, which is considerably ahead of the evening Post (143,000 daily, no Sunday edition).

Batavia:

> Parson Bldg., Batavia 45103
>
> (513) 732-1507, Steve Kemme

Columbus:

> 16 E. Broad St., Columbus 43215
>
> (614) 224-4640, Steve Wilson

Hamilton:

> 110 N. 3 St., Hamilton 45011
>
> (513) 863-2962, John Clark

Lebanon:

    8 S. Broadway, Lebanon 45036

    (513) 932-5278, James Rohrer

Middletown:

    1919 Central Ave., Middletown 45042

    (513) 424-0030, Irene Wright

Washington, D.C.:

    Box 7858, Wash., D.C. 20044

    (703) 276-5800 (Gannett Newspapers)

Indiana

Indianapolis:

    Suite 400, 150 W. Market St., Indianapolis 46204

    (317) 634-9751, Jeannine Guttman (Gannett News Service)

CINCINNATI POST

    800 Broadway, Cincinnati 45202

    (513) 352-2000

Columbus:

    41 S. High St., Columbus 43215

    (614) 228-1783, Maureen Brown

Covington, Ky.:

    421 Madison Ave., Covington 41011

    (606) 292-2600

    Editor Paul Knue is in charge of the Kentucky edition.

Washington, D.C.:

    1110 Vermont Ave., N.W., Wash., D.C. 20005

    (202) 833-9250, Jerry Condo

In addition to the Kentucky edition, the newspaper also publishes a suburban Valley edition, with a separate office in the Forest Hills area, at 629 Batavia Pike, Cincinnati 45244, (513) 528-1210; Susan Straub, editor. Circulation of the evening Post has decreased to 143,000.

Cincinnati is the central office of the Scripps-Howard Newspapers. The company no longer publishes The New York World Telegram & Sun, nor does it have outlets in Chicago or Los Angeles. Many publicists therefore are not aware of the huge size and importance of this newspaper group. The principal editorial office is the Scripps-Howard News Service bureau in Washington, D.C.

Syndicated columnists include Norman Nadel in New York and Ted Knapp in Washington. Distribution, via United Feature Syndicate, includes the 17 Scripps-Howard newspapers and others.

The Birmingham Post-Herald, Rocky Mountain News, Albuquerque Tribune, Columbus Citizen Journal, Pittsburgh Press, The Commercial Appeal and Memphis Press-Scimitar are each listed separately.

The other Scripps-Howard newspapers are the Hollywood Sun-Tattler and Stuart News in Florida, Evansville Press in Indiana, Knoxville News-Sentinel in Tennessee, El Paso Herald-Post in Texas, San Juan Star in Puerto Rico and The Daily News Tribune of Fullerton, Calif.

INDUSTRY WEEK

1111 Chester Ave., Cleveland 44114

(216) 696-7000

Chicago:

2 Illinois Center Bldg., Chicago 60601

(312) 861-0880, Brian Moskal

Los Angeles:

16255 Ventura Blvd., Encino 91436

(213) 990-9000, Lad Kuzela

New York:

122 E. 42 St., N.Y. 10168

(212) 867-9191, Marilyn Much

Pittsburgh:

3 Gateway Center, Pittsburgh 15222

(412) 281-8455, Donald B. Thompson

San Francisco:

1601 Bayshore Hwy., Burlingame 94010

(415) 692-1381, William Patterson

Washington, D.C.:

1030 15 St., N.W., Wash., D.C. 20005

(202) 223-6650, John S. McClenahen, William H. Miller

In addition to these bureau chiefs (called regional editors), Industry Week also has editorial correspondents in Birmingham, Boston, Cincinnati and Youngstown.

Penton/IPC, Inc., publishes other business and trade publications, including Air Transport World, Airconditioning and Refrigeration Business, Design Engineering, Foundry, Government Product News, Handling & Shipping Management, Hydraulics & Pneumatics, Lodging Hospitality, Machine Design, Material Handling Engineering, Modern Office Procedures, New Equipment Digest, Occupational Hazards, Power Transmission Design, Precision Metal, Restaurant Hospitality, School Product News, Welding Design & Fabrication and The Welding Distributor. Industry Week, a bi-weekly, has the largest circulation (259,000).

THE PLAIN DEALER

1801 Superior Ave., Cleveland 44114

(216) 344-4800

Ohio's largest circulation (up in 1983 to 493,000 daily, 501,000 Sunday), The P. D. appears on breakfast tables throughout the lakefront area.
Columbus:

16 E. Broad St., Columbus 43215

(614) 228-8200, Thomas Diemer

Lake county:

8 N. State St., Painesville 44077

(216) 357-6136, Karen Henderson

Washington, D.C.:

521 Ntl. Press Bldg., Wash., D.C. 20045

(202) 638-1366, Thomas Brazaitis

SUN NEWSPAPERS

5510 Cleveland Pkwy., Cleveland 44125

(216) 524-0830

This extraordinary chain of weekly newspapers (the actual name is Post Corporation Newspapers Group) consists of 18 weeklies (all published on Thursday) with a combined circulation of over 100,000 paid and over 100,000 free. Following are the seven offices. All are area code 216.
Beachwood:

23811 Chagrin Blvd., Beachwood 44122

464-6700, Arnold Rosenberg

(Sun Press, Sun Messenger)

Berea:

8 Berea Commons, Berea 44017

826-4460, Frank Waston

(News Sun, Strongville-N. Royalton Sun Star)

Brunswick:

811 Pearl Rd., Brunswick 44212

225-8110, Dennis Seeds

(Brunswick Sun Times, Medina Sun Sentinel)

Cleveland:

5510 Cloverleaf Pkwy. Cleveland 44125

524-0830, David Swiderski

(Parma Sun Post, West Side Sun News, Sun Courier, Garfield-Maple Heights Sun)

Euclid:

22630 Shore Center Dr., Euclid 44123

261-7650, John Urbancich

(Euclid Sun Journal, Sun Leader Journal, Sun Scoop Journal)

North Olmsted:
>
> 4707 West Northern Blvd., N. Olmsted 44070
>
> 777-3800, Michael McNulty
>
> (Lakewood Sun Post, Sun Herald)

Solon:
>
> 32914 Solon Rod., Solon 44139
>
> 349-0240, Ruth Wirtz
>
> (Chagrin Valley Herald Sun, Solon Herald Sun, Bedford Sun Banner)

CLEVELAND BUREAUS (area code 216)

Associated Press, Cleveland Plaza Hotel, 1127 Euclid Ave., Cleveland
44114, 771-2172

Business Week, 55 Public Square, Cleveland 44113, 781-7000

Fairchild Publications, Citizens Federal Tower, 2000 East 9 St., Cleveland
44115, 241-5940

Iron Age, 1717 E. 9 St., Cleveland 44114, George Weimet, 781-2860

United Press International, 401 Euclid Ave., Cleveland 44114, 771-3455

Wall Street Journal, 1325 Lakeside Ave., Cleveland 44114, Paul Ingrassia,
241-5183

COLUMBUS CITIZEN-JOURNAL

>
> 34 S. Third St., Columbus 43216
>
> (614) 461-5000

State Capital:
>
> 34 S. Third St., Columbus 43216
>
> (614) 461-5000, Dick Kimmins
>
> This bureau provides coverage in the state capital for the Scripps-

Howard Newspapers, the Cincinnati Post and Times-Star.

Washington, D.C.:
>
> 1110 Vermont Ave., N.W., Wash., D.C. 20005
>
> (202) 833-9250, Jerry Condo
>
> (Scripps-Howard Newspapers)

THE COLUMBUS DISPATCH

>
> 34 S. Third St., Columbus 4321
>
> (614) 461-5000

Washington, D.C.:
>
> 809 Ntl. Press Bldg., Wash., D.C. 20045
>
> (202) 347-3144, George Embrey

COLUMBUS BUREAUS (area code 614)

Akron Beacon Journal, 16 E. Broad St., Columbus 43215, William Hushey,
224-1613

Associated Press, Dispatch Bldg., 34 Third St., Columbus 43215, William
Di Mascio, 228-4306

Cincinnati Enquirer, 16 E. Broad St., Columbus 43215, Steve Wilson,
224-4640

Cincinnati Post, 41 S. High St., Columbus 43215, Maureen Brown,
228-1783

Cleveland Plain Dealer, 16 E. Broad St., Columbus 43215, Thomas Diemer,
228-8200

Dayton Daily News, Le Vegue Tower, Columbus 43215, Jim Ripley, 221-4939

Toledo Blade, 16 E. Broad St., Columbus 43215, Rick Kelly, 221-0496

United Press International, 50 W. Broad St., Columbus 43215, 221-4291

THE DAYTON DAILY NEWS

4th & Ludlow St., Dayton 45401

(513) 225-2237

Columbus:

LeVegue Tower, Columbus 43215

(614) 221-4939, Jim Ripley

Washington, D.C.:

1901 Pennsylvania Ave., N.W., Wash., D.C. 20006

(202) 331-0900, Tom Price (Cox Newspapers)

THE BLADE

541 Superior St., Toledo 43660

(419) 245-6000

Bowling Green:

215 Huntington Bank Bldg., 130 S. Main St., Bowling Green 43402

(419) 353-5972, Steve Pollick

Columbus:

16 E. Broad St., Columbus 43215

(614) 221-0496, Rick Kelly

Washington, D.C.:

1280 Ntl. Press Bldg., Wash., D.C. 20045

(202) 393-4580, Roland Powell

OKLAHOMA

THE DAILY OKLAHOMAN
OKLAHOMA CITY TIMES

Box 25125, Broadway & 4th St., Oklahoma City 73102

(405) 232-3311

The morning Oklahoman has the largest circulation in the state—187,000 and 296,000 on Sunday. The Times has the state's largest evening circulation (83,000). The newspapers merged in 1984.

Washington, D.C.:
>907 Ntl. Press Bldg., Wash., D.C. 20045
>
>(202) 628-0335, Allan W. Cromley

TULSA DAILY WORLD
>Box 1770, 315 S. Boulder Ave., Tulsa 74102
>
>(918) 583-2161

Oklahoma City:
>430 State Capitol, Oklahoma City 73105
>
>(405) 525-3311, Chuck Ervin

Washington, D.C.:
>1278 Ntl. Press Bldg., Wash., D.C. 20045
>
>(202) 347-8557, Malvina Stephenson

OREGON

EUGENE REGISTER-GUARD
>Box 10188, 975 High St., Eugene 97440
>
>(503) 485-1234

Lane County
>Box 613, Cottage Grove 97424, John Thompson
>
>Box 569, Florence 97439, Larry Bacon

Washington, D.C.:
>210 Seventh St., S.E., Wash., D.C. 20003
>
>(202) 543-1878, Steve Forrester

OREGON JOURNAL
>1320 S.W. Broadway, Portland 97201
>
>(503) 222-5511

Salem:
>Room 10, State Capitol, Salem 97310
>
>(503) 378-3026, Peter McConnell

Washington, D.C.:
>1750 Pennsylvania Ave., N.W., Wash., D.C. 20006
>
>(202) 298-7080, Joseph Berger
>
>(Newhouse News Service)

OREGONIAN

1320 S.W. Broadway, Portland 97201
(503) 221-8340

With the demise of the evening Oregon Journal in 1982, the Oregonian increased its circulation to 309,000 daily and 408,000 Sunday, which is the largest in the state. The Sunday circulation is one of the largest in the country. Several bureaus were opened to serve the booming area around Portland, including nearby Washington state.

Oregon
East Metro:

2053 E. Burnside, Gresham 97030
(503) 666-8100, Nancy McCarthy

South Metro:

Box 707, Oregon City 97045
(503) 656-0083, Jerry Boone

West Metro:

10245 S. W. Parkway, Portland 97225
(503) 297-8861, Diane Carman

Washington
North Metro:

208 W. 11th St., Vancouver 98660
(206) 694-1450, Lora Cuykendall

Washington, D.C.:

1750 Pennsylvania Ave., N. W., Wash., D.C. 20006
(202) 383-7825, Jim Flanigan, David Whitney
(Newhouse News Service)

PENNSYLVANIA

CALL-CHRONICLE

Box 1260, Allentown 18105
(215) 433-4241

Bethlehem:

509 Main St., Bethlehem 18018
(212) 865-5311, Edward Laepple

Bucks County:

West End Shopping Center, Quakers Town 18951
(215) 536-0601, J. Rollin Cressman

Easton:

1101 Northampton St., Easton 18402
(215) 258-3000, Terry Larimer

Harrisburg:
>	Box 1287, Harrisburg 17108
>	(717) 787-2067, Ben Livingood

Lehighton:
>	114 S. First St., Lehighton 18951
>	(215) 377-3530, Ray Conageski

Stroudsburg:
>	43 N. 7 St., Stroudsburg 18630
>	(215) 421-6500, Wealthy Kortz

Washington, D.C.:
>	316 Pennsylvania Ave., S.E., Wash., D.C. 20003
>	(202) 546-7500
>	(States News Service)

ERIE MORNING NEWS
ERIE DAILY TIMES
>	205 W. 12 St., Erie 16534
>	(814) 456-8531

The morning News (24,000) has a smaller circulation than the afternoon Times (49,000), which is unusual. Circulation of the Sunday Times-News is 96,000. The two newspapers are quite successful and are renowned for many achievements, including an extensive bureau system in western Pennsylvania. Fran Fry Jr., who is director of bureaus, is in the Franklin bureau.

Pennsylvania
Franklin:
>	1411 Liberty St., Franklin 16323
>	(814) 437-6397 (last 4 digits spell NEWS)
>	(Tri-City area)

Girard:
>	313 W. Main St., Girard 16417
>	(814) 774-4466
>	(East Erie county)

Hartborcreek:
>	1821B Nagel Rod., Erie 16510
>	(814 899-6397
>	(West Erie county)

Meadville:
>	812 Liberty St., Meadville 16335
>	(814) 724-5427

THE PATRIOT
THE EVENING NEWS
THE SUNDAY PATRIOT-NEWS
>   Box 2265, Ninth and Market Sts., Harrisburg 17105
>   (717) 2w55-8160
>   Central Pennsylvania area code is 717

Carlisle:
>   1 E. High St., Carlisle 17013
>   249-2006

Harrisburg:
>   State Capitol, Harrisburg 17101
>   787-3061, John Scotzin, Carmen Brutto

Hershey:
>   48 W. Caracas Ave., Hershey 17033
>   533-3257

Lebanon:
>   127 N. Ninth St., Lebanon 17042
>   272-3759

West Shore:
>   23rd and Market Sts., Camp Hill 1711
>   255-8225

York:
>   225 S. George St., York 17403
>   854-9524

Washington, D.C.:
>   1750 Pennsylvania Ave., N.W., Wash., D.C. 20006
>   (202) 383-7800, Robert Fichenberg
>   (Newhouse News Service)

HARRISBURG BUREAUS (area code 717)

Associated Press, 508 Payne-Shoemaker Bldg., 240 N. Third St., Harrisburg
>   17101, 238-9413

Call Chronicle, Box 1287, Harrisburg 17108, Ben Livingood, 787-2067

Philadelphia Inquirer, State Capitol, Box 1287, Harrisburg 17101, David
>   Morrison, 787-5934

Pittsburgh Post Gazette, State Capitol News Room, Harrisburg 17101, Jim
>   O'Loole, Gary Rothstein, 787-2141

Pittsburgh Press, State Capitol News Room, Harrisburg 17101, John Taylor,
>   787-6275

United Press International, 810 Payne-Shoemaker Bldg., 240 N. Third St.,
>   Harrisburg 17101, 234-4189

CHILTON PUBLICATIONS

Radnor 19089

(215) 964-4000

The Chilton magazines are:

Automotive Industries (also International)
Automotive Marketing
Commercial Car Journal
Distribution
Electronic Component News
Food Engineering Master
Food Engineering (also International)
Hardware Age
Instrument and Apparatus News
Instruments and Control Systems
Iron Age
Iron Age Metalworking International
Jewelers' Circular-Keystone
Motor Age
Owner Operator
Product Design & Development
Review of Optometry

The Chillton Washington bureau serves all of these publications:
1093 Ntl. Press Bldg., Wash., D.C. 20045

(202) 393-3473, Neil Regeimbal

In addition, several of the Chilton magazines maintain their own bureaus as follows:

AUTOMOTIVE INDUSTRIES

Chicago:

100 S. Wacker Drive, Chicago 60606

(312) 782-1400, John Furwalter

Detroit:

2600 Fisher Bldg., Detroit 48202

(313) 875-2090, Joseph Callahan, John McElroy

COMMERCIAL CAR JOURNAL

Detroit:

2600 Fisher Bldg., Detroit 48202

(313) 875-2090, Joseph Cobb

San Francisco:

24 White St., San Francisco 94109

(415) 474-8532, Ken MacDonald

FOOD ENGINEERING
Chicago:
> 100 S. Wacker Dr., Chicago 60606
> (312) 782-1400, Charles Morris

IRON AGE
Boston:
> 570 Hillside Ave., Needham Heights 02194
> (617) 444-0010, Raymond Larsen

Chicago:
> 100 S. Wacker Dr., Chicago 60606
> (312) 782-1400, Keith Bennett

Cleveland:
> 1717 E. 9 St., Cleveland 44114
> (216) 781-2860, George Weimet

Detroit:
> 2600 Fisher Bldg., Detroit 48202
> (313) 875-2090, B. H. Berry

Houston:
> 2500 Tanglewilde Ave., Houston 77063
> (713) 780-9620, S. T. Parker

Los Angeles:
> 6767 Forest Lawn Dr., L.A. 90068
> (213) 851-6500, A.M. Senia

New York:
> 825 Seventh Ave., N.Y. 10019
> (212)245-7555, Bob Regan

Pittsburgh:
> 1520 Park Bldg., Pittsburgh 15222
> (412) 281-1830, George McManus

PHILADELPHIA AREA

PHILADELPHIA INQUIRER
> 400 N. Broad St., Philadelphia 19101
> (215) 854-2500

> With the closing of the Philadelphia Bulletin on January 29, 1982, the Inquirer lost a major competitor. Daily circulation of the Inquirer now is 533,000, which is 10th largest in the U.S. and Sunday circulation is 995,000, which is sixth largest in the country.

Doylestown:
> Box 544, Doylestown 18901
> (215) 345-6043

Harrisburg:
>State Capitol, Box 1287, Harrisburg 17108
>(717) 787-5934, David Morrison

Langhorne:
>106 S. Bellevue Ave., Langhorne 19047
>(215) 757-0190, Russell Cooke

Lawrenceburg:
>202 W. High St., Lawrenceburg 47025
>(812) 537-0427, Caden Blincoe

Media:
>10 Veteran Square, Media 19063
>(215) 556-5422

Norristown:
>Montgomery Co. Courthouse, Airy & Swede Sts., Norristown 19401
>(215) 272-2707, Sara Schwoder
>Cherry & Ann Sts., Norristown 19401
>(215) 272-2707

Philadelphia City Hall:
>Room 309, 1 E. Penn Sq., Phila. 19107
>(215) 854-2958

Philadelphia Federal Court:
>6th & Market Sts., Room 2638, Phila. 19107
>(215) 854-2945, Jan Schaffer

Wayne:
>24 Lovella Court, Wayne 19087
>(215) 687-6101

West Chester:
>10 N. Church St., West Chester 19380
>(215) 431-7879, Stephan Salisbury

Delaware
Dover:
>Legislative Hall, Dover 19901
>(302) 678-9522

Wilmington:
>200 W. 9th St., Wilmington 19801
>(302) 656-3967, Greg Byrnes

New Jersey
Atlantic City:
>1 New York Ave., Atlantic City 08401
>(609) 344-2873, George Anastasia

Camden:

City Hall, Pressroom, Camden 08102

(609) 966-2722, Francis Lordon

Cherry Hill:

Heritage Bldg., 383 N. Kings Hwy., Cherry Hill 08003

(609) 667-6477, Dale Mezzacappa

Gloucester:

13 Curtis Ave., Woodbury 08021

(609) 848-4383, Jane Eisner

Mount Holly:

55 High St., Mt. Holly 08060

(609) 261-3200, Joyce Gemperlein

Trenton:

206 W. State St., Trenton 08608

(609) 989-8990, Lacy McCrary, John Hilferty

National

Los Angeles:

c/o L.A. Herald Examiner, Box 2416, Terminal Annex, L.A. 90051

(213) 749-1747, Larry Eichel

New York:

180 Riverside Dr., N.Y. 10024

(212) 787-3125, Barbara Kantrowitz

Washington, D.C.:

1319 F St., N.W. Wash., D.C. 20004

(202) 637-3600, Michael Hobbs

TV GUIDE

Radnor 19088

(215) 293-8500

Hollywood:

9000 Sunset Blvd, L.A. 90036

(213) 276-0676, Steve Gelman

New York:

1290 Avenue of the Americas, N.Y. 10019

(212) 484-9900, Neil Hickey

Washington, D.C.:

818 18th St., N.W., Wash., D.C. 20006

(202) 822-8632, John Weisman

TV Guide has a weekly circulation of about 17 million, with 106 editions. The outer feature pages are the same in all editions. Thus, the offices in cities other than Radnor, Los Angeles and New York are responsible only for obtaining program information.

PHILADELPHIA BUREAUS (area code 215)

Associated Press, Box 7784, Philadelphia 19101, George L. Zucher,
382-5571

Business Week, 3 Parkway, Philadelphia 19102, Robin Carlson, 568-6161

Fairchild Publications, WPVI-TV Bldg., 4100 City Line Ave., Philadelphia
19131, 879-8200

New York Times, 570 Lindsey Dr., Philadelphia 19087, William Robbins,
964-8828

United Press International, 1819 JFK Blvd., Suite 400, Philadelphia 19103,
563-6008

Wall Street Journal, 12 Broad St., Philadelphia 19107, Frank Allen, 893-4900

PITTSBURGH POST-GAZETTE

50 Blvd. of the Allies, Pittsburgh 15222
(412) 263-1100

Harrisburg:

Capitol News Room, Harrisburg 17101
(717) 787-2141, Jim O'Toole, Gary Rothstein

Washington, D.C.:

1280 Ntl. Press Bldg., Wash., D.C. 20045
(202) 393-4580, Jane Blotzer

The Block Newspapers include the Toledo Blade, Pittsburgh Post-Gazette, Red Bank (N.J.) Register, and Monterey (Calif.) Peninsula Herald. Headquarters are jointly maintained by Paul Block Jr., in Toledo, and William Block in Pittsburgh.

THE PITTSBURGH PRESS

34 Blvd. of the Allies, Pittsburgh 15230
(412) 263-1441

The Pittsburgh Press is exceptional in several ways. It is one of the few evening newspapers with a considerably larger circulation than its competing morning newspaper. The Press daily circulation is 255,000, as compared with the 177,000 of the Post-Gazette. Surprisingly, the morning P-G does not publish on Sundays, and the Press does. The result was a Sunday circulation in 1983 of 606,000, which is lower than in previous years but still is one of the largest in the country.

Harrisburg.

State Capitol News Room, Harrisburg 17108
(717) 787-6275, John Taylor

Washington, D.C.:

1110 Vermont Ave., N.W., Wash., D.C. 20005
(202) 833-9250, Kathy Kiely
(Scripps-Howard)

WILKES-BARRE CITIZENS' VOICE
>River & Market Sts., Wilkes-Barre 18711
>
>(717) 829-6854
>
>A morning newspaper, the Citizens' Voice has increased its coverage
in its suburban area.

Naticoke:
>133 E. Main St., Naticoke 18634
>
>(717) 735-3150, Curt Hules

Pittston:
>19 Broad St., Pittston 18640
>
>(717) 655-9641, Glen Hoffman

Plymouth:
>5 W. Main St., Plymouth 18651
>
>(717) 779-9571, William De Remer

Shavertown:
>Memorial Hwy., Shavertown 18708
>
>(717) 675-6522, William Jones

PITTSBURGH BUREAUS (area code 412)

Associated Press, 1111 Clark Bldg., 717 Liberty Ave., Pittsburgh 15222,
>281-3747

Business Week, 6 Gateway Center, Pittsburgh 15222, William Symonds,
>227-3640

Fairchild Publications, 2 Gateway Center, Pittsburgh 15222, 566-1260

Industry Week, 3 Gateway Center, Pittsburgh 15222, Donald B.
>Thompson, 281-8455

Iron Age, 1520 Park Bldg., Pittsburgh 15222, George McManus, 281-1830

USA Today, 1000 RIDC Plaza, Pittsburgh 15222, 963-0808

United Press International, Conestoga Blvd., 7 Wood St., Pittsburgh 15222,
>553-5300

Wall Street Journal, 1 Oliver Pl., Pittsburgh 15222, Dan Austin, 471-1904

RHODE ISLAND

THE PROVIDENCE EVENING BULLETIN
THE PROVIDENCE JOURNAL
>75 Fountain St., Providence 02902
>
>(401) 277-7300
>
>The Providence Journal-Bulletin maintains 12 bureaus in Rhode Island
and nearby Massachusetts.
>
>Of course, the Journal-Bulletin has the largest circulation of any
Rhode Island newspaper. There are only five other dailies, and their combined
circulation is about 100,000. The morning Journal has a circulation of 84,000;

the evening Bulletin has 135,000; the Saturday Journal-Bulletin has 194,000 and the Sunday Journal has 241,000. Since the population of Providence is about 157,000, this indeed is extraordinary. Furthermore, the 1983 circulation figures are considerably higher than in recent years.

Rhode Island
Blackstone Valley:

> 347 Main St., Pawtucket 02860
>
> 723-1020, Jack Khorey
>
> (Pawtucket, Central Falls, Cumberland, Lincoln)

East Bay:

> 504 Main St., Warren 02885
>
> 245-8600, David McCarthy
>
> (Bristol, Warren, Barrington, East Providence)

Greenville:

> Box 334, Hopkins Bldg., Greenville 02828
>
> 949-0900, Greg Smith
>
> (N. Providence, Johnston, Foster, Glocester, Smithfield, Scituate)

Newport:

> 170 Thames St., Newport 02840
>
> 846-0600, Elliot Krieger
>
> (Newport, Portsmouth, Middletown, Tiverton, Little Compton, Jamestown)

Pawtuxet Valley:

> 1167 Main St., W. Warwick 02893
>
> 821-8200, John B. Lake
>
> (W. Warwick, Coventry, W. Greenwich)

South County:

> Box 272, Quo Vadis Bldg., Wakefield 02879
>
> 783-3301, 884-3948, Gerald S. Goldstein
>
> (N. Kingston, S. Kingston, Exeter, Naragansett, Jamestown)

West Bay:

> 1837 Post Rd., Warwick 02866
>
> 737-3000, Mike Young
>
> (Warwick, Cranston, E. Greenwich)

Westerly:

> 1 Canal St., Westerly 02891
>
> 596-4911, Gregg Krupa
>
> (Westerly, Richmond, Hopkinton, Charlestown)

Wickford:

> 8234 Post Rd., N. Kingstown, RI 02852
>
> 294-4593, Gerald S. Goldstein
>
> (N. Kingstown)

Woonsocket:

    1 Social St., Woonsocket 02895

    762-2110, Bob Jagolinzer

    (Woonsocket, Burrillville, N. Smithfield)

Massachusetts (Eastern Massachusetts area code is 617)
Attleboro:

    Box 297, 1 Park St., Attleboro 02703

    222-8902, Don Sockol

    (Attleboro, N. Attleboro, Seekonk, Reheboth)
Fall River:

    Box 2572, 85 No. Main St., Fall River 02720

    674-8401, Edward J. Sullivan

    (Fall River, Somerset, Swansea)
Washington, D.C.:

    728 Ntl. Press Bldg., Wash., D.C. 20045

    (202) 628-6214, John Mulligan

SOUTH CAROLINA

THE COLUMBIA RECORD
THE STATE

    Box 1333, Stadium Road, Columbia 29202

    (803) 771-6161

    The morning State has the largest circulation in the state—103,000
daily and 138,000 Sunday. The evening Record has a circulation of 31,000.
Camden:

    Box 446, Camden 29202

    (803) 771-6161, Margaret B. Sprott
Florence:

    Box 1047, Florence 2950

    (803) 662-9691, Jerry Dyer
Newberry:

    Box 57, Newberry 29108

    (803) 276-9904, John G. Collins
Orangeburg:

    Box 291, Orangeburg 29116-0291

    (803) 536-9548, Gordon Hirsh
Washington, D.C.:

    6817 Old Stage Road, Rockville, MD 20852

    (301) 881-2220, Leland Bandy

THE GREENVILLE NEWS
GREENVILLE PIEDMONT
>Box 1688, Greenville 29602
>
>(803) 298-4100

The morning News has a circulation of 83,000; the afternoon Piedmont has a circulation of 23,000, and the Sunday News-Piedmont has a circulation of 111,000. The newspapers cover a large part of the state with correspondents in Anderson, Clemson, Clinton, Easley, Foundatin Inn, Greenwood, Greer, Laurens, Newberry, Pickens and Seneca, as well as a large bureau in Columbia.

Columbia:
>Box 11365, Columbia 29211
>
>(803) 779-2944, Chris Weston

SOUTH DAKOTA

SIOUX FALLS ARGUS-LEADER
>200 S. Minnesota, Sioux Falls 57102
>
>(605) 336-2200

Of the state's 12 newspapers, the Argus-Leader has the largest circulation—45,000 daily and 56,000 Sunday. The state is extraordinary in that it has only one morning newspaper, the Argus-Leader, which switched from evening publication in 1979.

Pierre:
>Box 1011, State Capitol Bldg., Pierre 57501
>
>(605) 224-2760, Rob Swenson

Washington, D.C.:
>1627 K St., N.W., Wash., D.C. 20006
>
>(202) 862-4900, John J. Curley (Gannett)

TENNESSEE

AMUSEMENT BUSINESS
>Box 24970, Nashville 37202
>
>(615) 748-8120

Chicago:
>150 N. Wacker Dr., Chicago 60606
>
>(312) 236-9818, Jim Helmer

Los Angeles:
>9107 Wilshine Blvd., L.A. 90210
>
>(213) 273-7040, Linda Deckard

New York:
>	1515 Broadway, N.Y. 10036
>	(212) 764-7300, Ancil Davis

THE CHATTANOOGA TIMES
>	117 E. 10 St., Chattanooga 37401
>	(615) 756-1234

Nashville:
>	Box 2566, Nashville 37219
>	(615) 255-0550, Nancy Hartis

THE COMMERCIAL APPEAL
>	495 Union Ave., Memphis 38101
>	(901) 529-2345

The morning Commercial Appeal has the state's largest circulation (200,000 daily and 283,000 Sunday). The evening Press-Scimitar ceased publication on October 31, 1983. The bureaus cover the tri-state area of Tennessee, Arkansas and Mississippi.

Arkansas:
>	1515 W. 7th, Little Rock 72202
>	(501) 372-2970, Guy Reel

Mississippi:
>	Box 22566, Jackson 39205
>	(601) 352-8631, James Young

Tennessee:
>	228 Capitol Bldg., Nashville 37219
>	(615) 255-4923, Richard Locker, J.W. Brosnan

Washington, D.C.:
>	1110 Vermont Ave., N.W., Wash., D.C. 20005
>	(202) 347-7750, Morris Cunningham, Mary Oeihel

The Washington bureau, which is part of the Scripps-Howard Newspaper Alliance, is interested in news about the mid-South, including Arkansas, western Kentucky, Mississippi, southeast Missouri and Tennessee. Walter Keazey is Tri-State Editor in the Memphis office.

NASHVILLE BANNER
>	1100 Broadway, Nashville 37202
>	(615) 259-8801
>	See listing under The Tennessean.

THE TENNESSEAN
>	1100 Broadway, Nashville 37202
>	(615) 255-1221

The morning Tennessean has the state's second largest circulation (134,000 daily, 242,000 Sunday). The evening Banner, which has the same ownership, has a daily circulation of 86,000.

Washington, D.C.:

>1000 Wilson Blvd., Arlington, VA 22209
>
>(703) 276-5800, Robert Dubill

TEXAS

ABILENE REPORTER-NEWS

>Box 30, 100 Block Cypress St., Abilene 79604
>
>(915) 673-4271

Austin:

>1122 Colorado, Austin 78701
>
>(512) 478-9644, Jim Davis (Harte-Hanks Communications)

Washington, D.C.:

>292 Ntl. Press Bldg., Wash., D.C. 20045
>
>(202) 628-1585, Bill Garland, Phil Swann
>
>(Hart-Hanks Communications)

AMARILLO GLOBE-NEWS

>Box 2091, 900 Harrison St., Amarillo 79166
>
>(806) 376-4488

Washington, D.C.:

>Suite 409, 236 Massachusetts Ave., N.E., Wash., D.C. 20002

THE AUSTIN AMERICAN-STATESMAN

>Box 670, Austin 78767
>
>(512) 445-3500

Capital:

>Press Room, State Capitol, Austin 78711
>
>(512) 445-3613, Bruce Hight

Washington, D.C.:

>1901 Pennsylvania Ave., N.W., Wash., D.C. 20006
>
>(202) 331-0900, Linda Simon

AUSTIN BUREAUS (area code 512)

Abilene Reporter-News, 1122 Colorado, Austin 78701, Jim Davis, 478-9644
Associated Press, Box 12247, Austin 78711, 472-4004
Corpus Christi Caller-Times, 1122 Colorado, Austin 78701, Jim Davis
Dallas Morning News, Box 12097, Austin 78711, George Kuempel, 478-5729
Dallas Times Herald, Box 12944, Austin 78711, Virginia Ellis Schmitt,
>478-7609

El Paso Times, Box 12964, Austin 78711, 476-4868
Fort Worth Star-Telegram, Box 12606, Austin 78711, Saralee Tiede, 476-4294
Houston Chronicle, Box 12307, Austin 78711, 478-3495
Houston Post, Box 12127, Austin 78711, Frelton West, 476-6557
San Antonio Express, San Antonio News, Box 13031, Austin 78711,
    Dick Merkel, 477-2650
San Antonio Light, Box 12368, Austin 78711, Edward Frills, 478-5663
United Press International, Box 12187, Austin 78711, 472-2471
Washington Post, Suite 645, Littlefield Bldg., Austin 78701, 473-2291

CORPUS CHRISTI CALLER-TIMES
Box 9136, Corpus Christi 78469
(512) 884-2011
Austin:
1122 Colorado, Austin 78701
(512) 478-9644, Jim Davis (Hart-Hanks)
Washington, D.C.:
292 Natl. Press Bldg., Wash., D.C. 20045
(202) 628-1585, Bill Garland (Harte-Hanks)

DALLAS MORNING NEWS
Communications Center, Dallas 75265
(214) 745-8222
The News had a 1983 circulation of 336,000 daily and 417,000 Sunday, an all-time high and considerably more than the rival News. In 1983, the News expanded its bureau system in the Dallas area and in the state and opened several national and international (Mexico and Israel) bureaus.

Metropolitan
Fort Worth:
1110 Executive Plaza Bldg., Ft. Worth 76102
(817) 336-3738, Dave Flick
Metro North
1547 Ave. K, Plano 75074
(214) 423-6461, Richard Connelly
Metro Northwest
4560 Beltline, Dallas 75234
(214) 458-2982, Jane Wolfe, Connie Pryzant
State
Austin:
Box 12097, Austin 79902
(512) 478-5729, George Kuempel

El Paso:

    4120 Rio Bravo St., El Paso 79902

    (915) 532-4408, John Gonzalez

Houston:

    932 Bankers Mortgage Bldg., 708 Main St., Houston 7700

    (713) 229-0008, Monica Reeves

San Antonio:

    705 E. Houston St., San Antonio 78205

    (512) 226-9083, David McLemore

East Texas:

    2737 S. Broadway, Tyler 75701

    (214) 595-4884, Steve Blow

National

New York:

    485 Lexington Ave., N.Y. 10017

    (212) 697-8145, Mike Geczi

Washington, D.C.:

    295 Natl. Press Bldg., Wash., D.C. 20045

    (202) 737-6127, Carl Leubsdorf

THE DALLAS TIMES HERALD

    1101 Pacific Ave., Dallas 75202

    (214) 744-6111

The all-day Times Herald, increased its circulation to 270,000 daily and 356,000 Sundays, all-time highs. Seven new bureaus were opened in 1983, an extraordinary expansion within the state. The newspaper aims to become one of America's most prominent, as indicated by the bureaus it has opened in New York, Cairo, Costa Rica and Mexico City, as well as its expanded bureau in Washington, D.C.

Austin:

    Box 12944, Capitol Station, Austin 78711

    (512) 478-7609, Virginia Ellis Schnitt

Collin County:

    1301 Summitt, Piano 75074

    (214) 424-2526, Beth Frerking

    (Ms. Frerking also covers Arlington, phone 817-860-9877).

Denton:

    914 N. Locust St., Denton 76201

    (817) 566-0593

El Paso:

    5812 Cromo Dr., El Paso 79912

    (915) 584-6673, Patrick McDonnell

Fort Worth:
>1116 Waggoner Bldg., 810 Houston St., Fort Worth 76102
>(817) 335-2108

Houston:
>Suite 959, Chronicle Bldg., 801 Texas Ave., Houston 77002
>(713) 222-8271, Tom Curtis

New York:
>Suite 1532, 26 Broadway, NY 10004
>(212) 422-7781, Janet Novack

San Antonio:
>2401 Tower Life Bldg., 310 S. St. Mary's, San Antonio 78205
>(512) 271-0654, Stuart Henigson

Tyler:
>1604 N. Bois d' Arc, Tyler 75702
>(214) 595-3391, Peter Larson

Valley:
>1135 E. Van Buren, Brownsville 78520
>(512) 544-4396

Washington, D.C.:
>559 Ntl. Press Bldg., Wash., D.C. 20045
>(202) 638-0404, Paul West

DALLAS BUREAUS (area code 214)

Advertising Age, 5327 N. Central Expy., Dallas 75205. Tom Buyer, 521-6650

Apparel News Group, 2300 Stemmons, Dallas 75258, Susan Roche, 634-8315

Associated Press, 2100 Southland Center, Dallas 75201, 742-3447

Aviation Week & Space Technology, 5151 Beltline Rd., Dallas 75240, Irwin Bulban, 458-2400

Business Week, 2001 Bryan Tower, Dallas 75201, Michael Sheldrick, 742-1747

Chemical Week, 907 Preston Wood Towers, 5151 Beltline Rd., Dallas 75249, Lorraine Smith, 458-2400

Chicago Tribune, 8350 N. Central Expy., Dallas 75206, Jim Coates, 373-0811

Electronics, 2001 Bryan Tower, Dallas 75201, J. Robert Tineback, 458-2400

Fairchild Publications, 2730 Stemmons Pkwy., Dallas 75207, Nina Flowinay, 630-5461

Gralla Publications, 15400 Knoll Trail Dr., Dallas 75248, 239-3060

McGraw-Hill World News Service, Suite 907, 5151 Beltline Rd., Dallas 75240, Lorraine Smith, 458-2400

Reuters, 442 Communications Ctr., Dallas 75265, David W. Finch, 698-9758

United Press International, 13900 Midway Rd., Dallas 75234, 980-8331

Wall Street Journal, 1233 Regal Row, Dallas 75247, Wayne Green, 631-7250

EL PASO TIMES

Box 20, El Paso 79999

(915) 546-6124

Located at the extreme western end of Texas, the El Paso Times has opened three new bureaus in nearby New Mexico, in addition to its bureau in Las Cruces.

Austin:

Box 12964, Austin 78711

(512) 476-4868

Alamogordo:

1517 Vermont Ave., Alamogordo, N.M. 88310

(505) 434-2204, David Sheppard

Carlsbad:

201 S. Halagueno, Carlsbad, N.M. 88220

(505) 885-0844, Marilyn Holmes

Las Cruces:

130 S. Waters, las Cruces, N.M. 88001

(505) 526-4211, Joan Morris

Sante Fe:

Box 2048, Santa Fe, NM 87501

(505) 988-2937, Doug McClellan

Washington, D.C.:

1627 K St., N.W., Wash., D.C. 20006

(202) 862-4900

FORT WORTH STAR-TELEGRAM

400 W. 7 St., Ft. Worth 76102

(817) 336-9271

Austin:

Box 12606, Capitol Sta., Austin 78711

(502) 476-4294, Saralee Tiede

Washington, D.C.:

1096 Ntl. Press Bldg., Wash., D.C. 20045

(202) 638-3107, Dave Montgomery

THE HOUSTON CHRONICLE

801 Texas Ave., Houston 77002

(713) 220-7171

The all-day Chronicle has the state's largest circulation, an all-time high in 1983 of 459,000 daily and 543,000 Sunday. The extremely successful newspaper is in the top five in the country in advertising lineage. The daily circulation is 15th largest in the country. Sunday circulation is 16th largest.

Austin:
>Box 12307, Capitol Station, Austin 78711
>(512) 478-3495

Washington, D.C.:
>1750 Pennsylvania Ave., N.W., Wash., D.C. 20006
>(202) 429-1990, Cragg Hines

HOUSTON POST

>4747 S.W. Freeway, Houston 77001
>(713) 621-7000

The morning Post, which is a vigorous competitor of the evening Chronicle, has considerably increased its daily circulation to 402,000 and Sunday circulation to 463,000 (behind the Chronicle and second biggest in the state).

Austin:
>Box 12127, Austin 78711
>(512) 476-6557, Felton West

Galveston:
>Box 3405, Galveston 77550
>(713) 762-9656, Steve Olafson

Washington, D.C.:
>291 Ntl. Press Bldg., Wash., D.C. 20045
>(202) 638-4332, Jim Craig

MEDICAL WORLD NEWS

>7676 Woodway, Houston 77063
>(713) 780-2299

Medical World News was sold by McGraw-Hill and transferred its headquarters from New York to Houston.

Chicago:
>1143 West Pratt, Chicago 60626
>(312) 274-6580, Judy Alsenfrom

Los Angeles:
>3612 Hamilton St., Irvine, CA 92714
>(714) 552-4481, Richard Trubo

New York:
>211 E. 43 St., N.Y. 10017
>(212) 490-7817, Malcolm Manber, Rochelle Green

San Francisco:
>40 Lansing St., San Francisco 94105
>(415) 777-3208, Judy Ismach

Washington, D.C.:
>Box 53414, Wash., D.C. 20009
>(202) 737-1171, 737-1078, Don Gibbons, Fran Pollner

HOUSTON BUREAUS (area code 713)

Associated Press, 609 Fannin Street, Houston 77002, 236-8181

Business Week, 375 Dresser Tower, Houston 77002, James Norman,
>659-1692

Chemical & Engineering News, Box 27620, Houston 77027, Bruce Greek,
>522-4125

Chemical Week, 375 Dresser Tower, 601 Jefferson St., Houston 77002, Eric
>Johnson, 659-4558

Dallas Morning News, 932 Bankers Mortgage Bldg., 708 Main Street,
>Houston 77002, Monica Reeves, 229-0008

Dallas Times Herald, Suite 959, Chronicle Bldg., 801 Texas Ave., Houston
>77002, Tom Curtis, 222-8271

Fairchild Publications, Suite 853, 801 Texas Ave., Houston 77002,
>223-0194

Forbes, 2 Shell Plaza Bldg., Houston 77002, William Baldwin, 228-2800

Fortune, 914 Main St., Houston 77002, Alexander Stuart, 759-9499

Iron Age, 2500 Tanglewood Ave., Houston 77063, S.T. Parker, 780-9620

Journal of Commerce, 1520 World Trade Bldg., Houston 77002,
>Stanley Mantrop, 227-8670

Los Angeles Times, Chronicle Bldg., Houston 77002, Rone Tempest,
>237-0808

McGraw-Hill World News Service, 375 Dresser Tower, 601 Jefferson St.,
>Houston 77002, Eric Johnson, 659-4558

New York Times, 801 Congress St., Houston 77002, Wayne King, 227-2638

Newsweek, Pennzoil Place, South Tower, 711 Louisiana, Houston 77002,
>Stryher McGuire, 227-2411

Penthouse, 1913 Gardenia St., Houston 77018, Kent Demaret, 681-0478

Reuters, 1 Allen Center, Houston 77002, Allen Van Cranelbrock, 659-2450

Time, 1125 Commerce Bldg., 914 Main Street, Houston 77002, David Jackson
>759-0907

U.S. News & World Report, 1965 Texas Commerce Tower, Houston 77002,
>Joseph Benham, Sarah Peterson, 227-5688

United Press International, 708 Main Street, Houston 77002, 227-2171

Wall Street Journal, 2770 Texas Commerce Towers, 601 Travis Street,
>Houston 77002, George Getschow, 227-5440

SAN ANTONIO EXPRESS
SAN ANTONIO NEWS

Box 2171, San Antonio 78297

(512) 477-2650

Austin:

Box 13031, Capitol Station, Austin 78711

(512) 477-2650, Dick Merkel

Washington, D.C.:

533 Natl. Press Bldg., Wash., D.C. 20045

(202) 313-1531, Niles Lathem

SAN ANTONIO LIGHT

Box 161, Broadway at McCullough, San Antonio 78291

(512) 271-2700

Austin:

Box 12368, Capitol Station, Austin 78711

(512) 478-5663, Edward Fills

Washington, D.C.:

510 First Ntl. Bank Bldg., 1701 Pennsylvania Ave., N.W., Wash., D.C. 20006

(202) 298-6920

(Hearst Newspapers)

UTAH

DESERET NEWS

Box 1257, 30 E. First St., Salt Lake City 84110

(801) 237-2100

The evening Deseret News is nationally known and highly respected, in spite of the perhaps surprising fact that its circulation (76,000) is considerably less than the morning Tribune.

Regional editions are published, and Richard Hall is regional editor, at the main office.

(Utah area code is 801)

Cedar City:

475 S. 940 West, Cedar City 84720

586-6870, Afton S. LeFevre

Logan:

165 N. 2nd West, Logan 84321

752-9353, Tim Gurrister

Ogden:

1470 Darling, Ogden 84403

393-6922, Barbara Bernstein

Utah County:
> 1 E. Center St., Provo 84601
> 374-1172, Kris Radish

Richfield:
> 475 W. 5 North, Richfield 84701
> 869-4459, Reed L. Madsen

Washington, D.C.:
> 1502 Stonewall Rd., Alexandria, VA 22302
> (703) 683-4019, Gordon E. White

VIRGINIA

THE ALEXANDRIA GAZETTE

> 717 N. Saint Asaph St., Alexandria 22313
> (703) 549-0004

An evening newspaper (circulation 11,000), the Gazette has a larger circulation than the morning Journal (published by a division of Army Times). The Gazette was established in 1784 and claims to be the oldest daily newspaper in the United States. However, the Hartford Courant was established in 1764. The Gazette also publishes three successful weeklies, the Burke Herald, Fairfax Tribune and Springfield Independent. All are published in Alexandria with no bureaus.

USA TODAY

> 100 Wilson Blvd., Arlington 22209
> (703) 276-3400
> See listing under District of Columbia

THE VIRGINIAN-PILOT AND THE LEDGER-STAR

> 150 W. Brambleton Ave., Norfolk 23501
> (804) 446-2000

Virginia (all are area code 804)

Chesapeake:
> 921 N. Battlefield Blvd., Chesapeake 23320
> 547-0088, Ronald L. Speer

Plymouth:
> 355 Crawford Pky., Portsmouth 23704
> 446-2612, Ed Rogers

Richmond:
> 508 Heritage Bldg., 10th & Main Sts., Richmond 23219
> 648-7785

Suffolk:
> 101 Saratoga St., Suffolk 23434
> 934-2335, John Pruitt

Virginia Beach:

> 4565 Virginia Beach Blvd., Va. Beach 23462
>
> 490-2337, Dennis hartig

North Carolina

Ahoskie:

> Box 523, Ahoskie 27910
>
> (919) 332-4043

Elizabeth City:

> Kramer Bldg., Elizabeth City 27909
>
> (919) 338-0159

The morning Virginian-Pilot and evening Ledger-Star are published by Landmark Communications, Inc., which also publishes the Greensboro News and The Greensboro Record in North Carolina and the Roanoke Times & World News in Virginia.

The Pilot and Ledger serve the cities of Norfolk, Portsmouth, Chesapeake, Virginia Beach and Suffolk on the south side of Hampton Roads harbor in southeastern Virginia. The Pilot also covers the southside counties of Southampton and Isle of Wight, Virginia's Eastern Shore and Northeastern North Carolina, including the Outer Banks.

In addition, published with the Pilot and Ledger two to three times a week are tabloid community news supplements for each of the five major cities. The supplements are: Norfolk Compass, Portsmouth Currents, Chesapeake Clipper, Virginia Beach Beacon and Suffolk Sun. The supplement offices are in the bureaus serving their respective cities.

RICHMOND TIMES-DISPATCH

> 333 E. Grace St., Richmond 23219
>
> (804) 649-6000

The morning Times-Dispatch has the state's largest circulation, 137,000 daily, 230,000 Sunday. Richmond Newspapers also publishes the evening News Leader (115,000).

Virginia

Charlottesville:

> Box 381, 416 E. Jefferson St., Charlottesville 22901
>
> (804) 295-9542, Carlos Santos

Clarkesville:

> Box 1177, Clarksville 23928
>
> (804) 374-2311, John Huke

Fredericksburg:

> Box 3365, 608 Williams St., Fredericksburg 22401
>
> (703) 371-4792, Ron Sauder

Petersburg:

> Box 342, 20 E. Tabb St., Petersburg 23803
>
> (804) 861-1576, Richard E. Gordon

Southside:

>Box 783, Victoria 23974
>
>(804) 696-2227, John Clement

Staunton:

>Box 846, 13 W. Beverly St., Staunton 24401
>
>(703) 886-2839, Gail Nardo

Warsaw (Northern Neck):

>Box 151, 111 E. Richmond Rd., Warsaw 22572
>
>(804) 333-3461, Albert Oetgen

Williamsburg:

>Box 439, Wilson Bldg., Duek of Gloucester St., Williamsburg 23185
>
>(804) 229-1512, Wilford Kale

The Richmond Times-Dispatch, an affiliate of Media General, covers a large part of Virginia with these bureaus, under the supervision of Thomas W. Howard, state editor, (804) 649-6341. Note that the state of Virginia formerly was one telephone area code and now is divided into two areas, 703 and 804, with Richmond in the 804 area. The newspaper also maintains a Washington, D.C., bureau:

>214 Ntl. Press Bldg., Wash., D.C. 20045
>
>(202) 347-7770, John Hall

The Washington bureau serves the Media General newspapers in Richmond; Tampa, Fla., and Winston-Salem, N.C.

ROANOKE TIMES & WORLD-NEWS

>Box 2491, Roanoke 24010
>
>(703) 891-3341

New River Valley:

>Box 416, Christianburg 27073
>
>(703) 382-4905, Charles Burress

Piedmont:

>1001 E. Main St., Richmond 23219
>
>(804) 643-2257, Margie Fisher

Salem:

>10 College Ave., S., Salem 24153
>
>(703) 389-4247

Shenandoah Valley:

>Drawer 1529, Lexington 24450
>
>(703) 463-9398, Mary Bishop

Southwest Virginia:

>Box 185, Wytheville 24382
>
>(703) 228-4752, Paul Dellinger

WASHINGTON

SEATTLE POST-INTELLIGENCER
Sixth & Wall St., Seattle 98111
(206) 628-8000
Olympia:
Rt. 6, Box 424, Olympia 98501
(206) 943-3990, Mike Layton
Washington, D.C.:
510 First Ntl. Bank Bldg., 1701 Pennsylvania Ave., N.W., Wash., D.C.
20006, (202) 659-2560, Joseph Kingsbury Smith
(Hearst Newspapers)

THE SEATTLE TIMES
Fairview Ave. No. and John St., Box 70, Seattle 98111
(206) 464-2111
The evening Times has the state's largest circulation (230,000). In
1983, the Times and Post-Intelligencer joined to produce a Sunday edition,
which now has a circulation of 490,000, one of the largest in the country.
Eastside:
10843 N.E. 8 St., Bellevue 98004
(206) 464-2182
Northend:
19730 64 Ave., W., Lynwood 98036
(206) 775-1959
Olympia:
c/o UPI, Legislative Bldg., Olympia 98501
(206) 943-9878
Southend:
6000 Southcenter Bldg., Tukwila 98188
(206) 464-2475
Washington, D.C.:
318 6 St., N.E., Wash., D.C. 20002
(202) 543-4386, Ross Anderson

THE TACOMA NEWS TRIBUNE
Box 11000, Tacoma 98411
(206) 597-8686
Olympia:
1417 S. Columbia St., Olympia 98504
(206) 352-0212, Robert Cummings

THE COLUMBIAN
Box 180, Vancouver 98666
(206) 694-3391
No bureaus.

WEST VIRGINIA

THE CHARLESTON GAZETTE AND MAIL
1001 Virginia St., E. Charleston 25330
(304) 348-5100
The morning Gazette and evening Mail each have a circulation of about 56,000, which is the largest in the state. The Sunday Gazette-Mail has a circulation of 107,000.

Raleigh-Fayette counties:
110 Poplar St., Beckley 25801
(304) 252-4874, Mrs. Opal Ripley

WHEELING INTELLIGENCER
1500 Main St., Wheeling 26003
(304) 233-0100
New Martinsville:
New Martinsville 26155
(304) 455-2662
Moundsville:
Moundsville 26041
(304) 845-3603, David Sedore
Steubenville-Weirton:
215 N. 5 St., Steubenville 43952
(614) 282-3601, Ann Koon
Eastern Ohio:
1500 Main St., Wheeling, WV 26003
(304) 233-0100, Bill Speer

WISCONSIN

GREEN BAY PRESS-GAZETTE
Box 430, 435 E. Walnut St., Green Bay 54305
(414) 435-4411
Washington, D.C.:
1000 Wilson Blvd., Arlington, VA 22209
(703) 276-5800, Robert Dubill (Gannett)

WISCONSIN STATE JOURNAL

Box 8058, Madison 53708

(607) 252-6100

Formerly located in the center of the city near the state capitol, Madison Newspapers, Inc. now is at 1901 Fish Hatchery Rd. The company publishes the morning Journal (71,000 daily and 126,000 Sundays) and in the evening, the Capital Times (32,000), which are vigorously independent of each other. No bureaus.

THE MILWAUKEE JOURNAL

333 W. State St., Milwaukee 53201

(414) 224-2000

The evening Journal has the state's largest circulation, 303,000 and is one of the country's most respected newspapers (24th largest). Sunday circulation is 524,000, 18th largest in the country. The morning Sentinel (180,000, second biggest in the state) is owned by The Journal Co., but it has a completely separate editorial operation at a different address. The Sentinel formerly was a Hearst newspaper.

Madison:

23 N. Pinckney St., Madison 53703

(608) 256-2553, Ron Elving

Waukesha:

720 N. East Ave., Milwaukee 5

(414) 547-2792, Dan Hanley

Washington, D.C.:

259 Ntl. Press Bldg., Wash., D.C. 20045

(202) 737-2985, John W. Kole

THE MILWAUKEE SENTINEL

Box 371, 918 N. 4 St., Milwaukee 53201

(414) 224-21

A division of The Journal Co., the morning Sentinel differs from most morning newspapers in that it is not the dominant newspaper in its area. However, 1983 circulation increased to 180,000. The Sentinel indeed is a major statewide newspaper.

Madison:

110 E. Main St., Madison 53703

(608) 255-5000, Neil Shively

Ozaukee:

166 W. Grand Ave., Port Washington 53074

(414) 284-2604

Racine:

> 302 6th St., Racine 53400
>
> (414) 637-0546

Waukesha:

> Waukesha Courthouse, 515 W. Moreland Blvd., Waukesha 53186
>
> (414) 542-0340, Richard Ferer

Washington, D.C.:

> 1290 Ntl. Press Bldg., Wash., D.C. 20045
>
> (202) 628-8920, Richard Bradee

WYOMING

CASPER STAR-TRIBUNE

> 170 Star Lane, Casper 82602
>
> (307) 266-0500
>
> The morning Star-Tribune has the largest circulation (38,000 daily, 41,000 Sunday) of the 10 daily newspapers in the state.

Cheyenne:

> State Capitol Bldg., Cheyenne 82001
>
> (307) 632-1244

THE SALT LAKE CITY TRIBUNE

> Box 867, 143 S. Main St., Salt Lake City 84110
>
> (801) 237-2011
>
> The morning Tribune is the largest circulation (112,000 daily, 180,000 Sunday) of the state's six daily newspapers. The Tribune has bureaus but prefers to channel news through the city editor.

Washington, D.C.:

> 13514 Duhart Rd., Germantown, MD 20874
>
> (301) 972-4140, Tom Gorey

VERMONT

THE BURLINGTON FREE PRESS

191 College St., Burlington 05401

(802) 863-3411

The morning Free Press has the largest circulation (51,000 daily, 49,000 Sunday) of the state's 10 daily newspapers. Vermont newspapers are different from most other states. Of the 10 dailies, six are afternoon newspapers. Only five of the ten dailies publish on Sunday. Sunday circulation generally is more than during the week; this is not the case with the Free Press, as a result of competition from the Boston and New York newspapers.

Capital Bureau:

Thrush Tavern, Box 307, Montpelier 05602

(802) 229-9141, Neil Davis

For Washington, D.C., and other bureaus, see Gannett Newspapers.

INDEX